Ten Years on a Georgia Plantation Since the War

By

Mrs. Frances B. Leigh

NEGRO UNIVERSITIES PRESS

NEW YORK

Originally published in 1883, London

Reprinted 1969 by
Negro Universities Press
A DIVISION OF GREENWOOD PUBLISHING CORP.
NEW YORK

SBN 8371-1177-3

PRINTED IN UNITED STATES OF AMERICA

BROTHERS AGAIN:

SUGGESTED BY DECORATION DAY, 1877.

—◦◇◦—

I.

Great Land! of all thy children 'tis the part
To give themselves to thee, to shelter thee,
To live for thee, and love with their whole heart,
Or die for thy fair fame, if needs must be :
And of thy children, both from South and North,
Some went to battle called in thousands forth
By thy dear voice, and conquered, though they
 died;
And some, who heard indeed that solemn call,
But wrongly heard, fell on a vanquished side,
Yet well contented for that side to fall ;
Brothers with brothers fought, and in that fight
Let all rejoice who fell, still thinking they were
 right.

II.

I wandered slowly through a far off-town,
Where the white winter comes not, nor the storm
Lashes with icy scourge fair flowers down
To early graves ; where balmy winds disarm
The wrathful tempest's rage ; and as I went,
Sudden I came upon a monument.
Inscribed was this : *To the Confederate Dead :*
And underneath, the period of the strife,—
Those four dire years that dashed away the life,
The life of priceless thousands, and o'erspread
Our land with mourning ;—on the other side
Only these words : ' *Come from the four winds, O
     Breath,*
And breathe upon these slain that they may live : '
No bitterness, no anger, naught beside
A sigh of silence, unexpressed, that saith
Of sorrow more than tears could weep, loud grief
     could give.

III.

Then the whole story of the war, methought,
Passed in its dreary length from first to last,—
By those great words into my memory brought,
Summoned from out the pages of the past.
An April dawn, near ninety years before,
Had seen a horseman in the shadowy night

Flit through New England's towns announcing war,
Calling the stout old patriots out to fight :—
An April dawn saw that first crashing shell
Rush through the startled air, and thundering
    burst
On Sumter's head ; and as it shattering fell,
The herald sound shrieked discord. This the last
Alarm of strife, and then in dark array
Battle on battle followed, fray on fray :
Name after name, in stern succession falling,
Bears with it countless tales of blood and woe ;
What countless others, mournful, sad, appalling,
Must silent rest, with voices silent too !
What multitudes of heroes now are resting
Unknown beneath the sod where first they fell !
And slander's tongue their name has ceased molest-
    ing,—
Has let them lie untroubled where they fell ;
While through the country each name with it bears
A memory of triumph or of tears.
Sadly to hearts bereaved they now must sound,
Beginning with themselves a life-long grief,
Recalling as each separate year comes round
Some sorrow borne alone beyond relief.
See quiet Williamsburg, where swaying shade
O'erspreads the tree-girt college ; fire and blood
In all their ghastly shapes her halls invade,
While flames resistless scar the scorching wood.
High soars the blaze, nor deigns on earth to tread,

But flies remorseless o'er the silent dead.
Above that fitful glare the leaden sky
Grows lurid at the sight of agony,
Till darker ever as the cloud descends
Heaven pours the flood, and night the horror ends.
Then followed seasons when the deadly heat
Fell in its fury on the parching earth,
And on the springing crops resistless beat,
Bearing a time of drought, a time of dearth :
Then gloomy Autumn, dismal with its rains,
A weary time, when our fair nation's brow
Was racked with sorrow, while on marshy plains
Still poured her life-blood, still increased her woe ;
Huge swamps extended o'er the tedious track,
And rivers rose, and pestilence was shed
On saddened ranks, and as report came back
Of some new fight, of some new hero dead,
Our land was forced to weep upon the graves
Of sons unnatural, of erring braves.
Still the grim trump of war, whose thrilling blast
Shaketh the battlements of peace, whose shock
Has made our country reel, its summons cast
Forth to the skies, and to the battle smoke
Marshalled both young and old, and wider through
Both North and South the desolation grew.
Up to the Northern gates the contest surges,
And three long days at Gettysburg runs high :
Out went both young and old ; the funeral dirges
Blend with the glorious chant of victory.

Three fearful days beneath the burning sun !
What hopes soared up, and fell, ere they were done !
And when the twilight bless'd came gently creep-
    ing,
For the third time over that bloody scene,
Where their last slumber gallant forms were sleep-
    ing
On hills that once, alas ! were fair and green—
When in that night of stillness, sad, serene,
Fond mothers sought their voiceless sons with
    weeping,
And sounds of nature sang a solemn song
Through the deep woods, and rushing brooks
    along—
Then was the land in the abysm of war,
Yet still, how long a time ere it was o'er !

IV.

Here the grim picture on my sight
Crowded too swift to sec each fight,
But in the darkness of the night,
   The Wildcrness I saw ;
And fighting forms and charging lines—
Or in the dusk the beacon signs
As through the wood the watch-fire shines,
   And skulking foes withdraw :—
Swift and more swift the pageant moves,
Now climbing hills, and now in groves,

Now on some blasted heath,
While still the lurid smoke and glare
Cover the sky and choke the air,
    Leaving their work beneath ;
For all along that weary way
The dead and dying scattered lay.
And so proceeding to the close,
    They fight, and fall, and die,
Until no more the watch-fire glows,
    Nor swells the battle cry :
'Tis done ;—the dead are now at rest
Upon their country's rugged breast.

V.

The wild bird builds her nest in branches tall,
Amid the sheltering foliage of the tree
Whose life was shattered by the deadly ball
That crashed its green boughs once so ruthlessly :
The wild bird sings his carol o'er the graves
Of many fallen heroes where the grass
Has grown, or where the ceaseless murmuring
    waves
The site of some past conflict scarce can trace :
If Nature thus, with all her healing arts,
Hath striven to smooth the furrows from the breast
Of our dear land, should we not do our best
To smooth all furrows from our wounded hearts ?
Then let us pray that as the sun and showers

Have charmed with their soft spell the dreary
    scenes,
Till scarce they know themselves through all the
    flowers
Strewn in their brakes and on their sloping greens,
So we may let the showers of Lethe flow
Upon the memory of that time of woe.

VI.

Shade-wrapped Savannah! By thy monument
A lesson hath been taught to great and small,
O may thy prayers be heard, its answer sent,
Granted by Heaven's grace unto us all!
And when th' Eternal breath shall come at last,
Breathing upon the land and summoning
From all the battle-field an army vast,
And by its power from every region bring
Both young and old, from every sepulchre
On mountain side, by stream and forest brake,
And shall along the moaning ocean stir,
Causing our dead from their long sleep to wake—
The soldiers shall arise, mingled in death,
And come together to the throne all bright,
Each to be judged according to his light,
Made perfect by that Great All-healing Breath;
No strife, no rancour, nothing bitter then,
But they shall join their hands Brothers again.

                    O. W.

TEN YEARS

ON

A GEORGIA PLANTATION.

———⋄———

CHAPTER I.

CHAOS.

THE year after the war between the North
and the South, I went to the South with my
father to look after our property in Georgia
and see what could be done with it.

The whole country had of course under-
gone a complete revolution. The changes
that a four years' war must bring about in any
country would alone have been enough to
give a different aspect to everything; but at
the South, besides the changes brought about
by the war, our slaves had been freed; the

white population was conquered, ruined, and
disheartened, unable for the moment to see
anything but ruin before as well as behind,
too wedded to the fancied prosperity of the
old system to believe in any possible success
under the new. And even had the people
desired to begin at once to rebuild their
fortunes, it would have been in most cases
impossible, for in many families the young
men had perished in the war, and the old
men, if not too old for the labour and effort
it required to set the machinery of peace
going again, were beggared, and had not even
money enough to buy food for themselves
and their families, let alone their negroes, to
whom they now had to pay wages as well as
feed them.

Besides this, the South was still treated
as a conquered country. The white people
were disfranchised, the local government in
the hands of either military men or Northern
adventurers, the latter of whom, with no
desire to promote either the good of the

country or people, but only to advance their own private ends, encouraged the negroes in all their foolish and extravagant ideas of freedom, set them against their old masters, filled their minds with false hopes, and pandered to their worst passions, in order to secure for themselves some political office which they hoped to obtain through the negro vote.

Into this state of things we came from the North, and I was often asked at the time, and have been since, to write some account of my own personal experience of the condition of the South immediately after the war, and during the following five years. But I never felt inclined to do so until now, when, in reading over a quantity of old letters written at the time, I find so much in them that is interesting, illustrative of the times and people, that I have determined to copy some of my accounts and descriptions, which may interest some persons now, and my children hereafter. Soon everything will be so changed, and the old traits of the negro slave have so entirely vanished, as to make stories about them sound like tales of a lost race ; and also because even now, so little is really known of the state of things politically at the South.

The accounts which have been written from time to time have been written either by travellers, who with every desire to get at the truth, could but see things superficially, or by persons whose feelings were too strong either on one side or the other to be perfectly just in their representations. I copy my impressions of things as they struck me then, although in many cases later events proved how false these impressions were, and how often mistaken I was in the opinions I formed. Indeed, we very often found ourselves taking entirely opposite views of things from day to day, which will explain apparent inconsistencies and contradictions in my statements ; but the new and unsettled condition of everything could not fail to produce this result, as well as the excited state we were all in.

I mention many rumours that reached us, which at the time we believed to be true, and which sometimes turned out to be so, but as often, not, as well as the things I know to be facts from my own personal experience, for rumours and exaggerations of all kinds made in a great measure the interest and excitement of our lives, although the reality was strange and painful enough.

On March 22, 1866, my father and myself left the North. The Southern railroads were many of them destroyed for miles, not having been rebuilt since the war, and it was very questionable how we were to get as far as Savannah, a matter we did accomplish however, in a week's time, after the following adventures, of which I find an account in my letters written at the time. We stopped one day in Washington, and went all over the new Capitol, which had been finished since I was there five years ago.

On Saturday we left, reaching Richmond at four o'clock on Sunday morning. I notice that it is a peculiarity of Southern railroads that they always either arrive, or start, at four o'clock in the morning. That day we spent quietly there, and sad enough it was, for besides all the associations with the place which crowded thick and fast upon one's memory, half the town was a heap of burnt ruins, showing how heavily the desolation of war had fallen upon it. And in the afternoon I went out to the cemetery, and after some search found the grave I was looking for. There he lay, with hundreds of others who had sacrificed their lives in vain, their resting place marked merely by small wooden headboards, bearing their names, regiments, and the battles in which they fell. The grief and excitement made me quite ill, so that I was glad to leave the town before daylight the next morning, and I hope I may never be there again.

We travelled all that day in the train,

reaching Greensborough that night at eight o'clock. Not having been able to get any information about our route further on, we thought it best to stop where we were until we did find out. This difficulty was one that met us at every fresh stopping place along the whole journey; no one could tell us whether the road ahead were open or not, and, if open, whether there were any means of getting over it. So we crawled on, dreading at each fresh stage to find ourselves stranded in the middle of the pine woods, with no means of progressing further.

That night in Greensborough is one never to be forgotten. The hotel was a miserable tumble-down old frame house, and the room we were shown into more fit for a stable than a human habitation ; a dirty bare floor, the panes more than half broken out of the windows, with two ragged, dirty calico curtains over them that waved and blew about in the wind. The furniture consisted of a bed, the clothes of which looked as if they had not been changed since the war, but had been slept in, in the meanwhile, constantly, two rickety old chairs, and a table with three legs. The bed being entirely out of the question, and I very tired, I took my bundle of shawls, put them under my head against the wall, tilted my chair back, and prepared to go to sleep if I could. I was just dozing off when I heard my maid, whom I had kept in the room for protection, give a start and exclamation which roused me. I asked her what was the matter, to which she replied, a huge rat had just run across the floor. This woke me quite up, and we spent the rest of the night shivering and shaking with the cold, and knocking on the floor with our umbrellas to frighten away the rats, which from time to time came out to look at us.

At four in the morning my father came for us, and we started for the train, driving two miles in an old army ambulance. From that time until eight in the evening we did not leave the cars, and then only left them to get into an old broken-down stage coach, which was originally intended to hold six people, but into which on this occasion they put nine, and, thus cramped and crowded, we drove for five hours over as rough a road as can well be imagined, reaching Columbia at three o'clock A.M., by which time I could hardly move. Our next train started at six, but I was so stiff and exhausted that I begged my father to wait over one day to rest, to which he consented. At this place we struck General Sherman's track, and here the ruin and desolation was complete. Hardly any of the town remained ; street after street was merely one long line of blackened ruins, which showed from their size and beautifully laid-out gardens, how handsome some of the houses had been. It was too horrible !

On Thursday, at six A.M., we again set off, going about thirty miles in a cattle van which brought us to the Columbia River, the bridge over which Sherman had destroyed. This we crossed on a pontoon bridge, after which we walked a mile, sat two hours in the woods, and were then picked up by a rickety old car which was backed down to where we were, and where the rails began again, having been torn up behind us.   In this, at the rate of about five miles an hour, we travelled until four in the afternoon, when we were again deposited in the woods, the line this time being torn up in front of us.   Here, after another wait, we were packed into a rough army waggon, with loose boards put across for seats, and in which we were jolted and banged about over a road composed entirely of ruts and roots for four more hours, until I thought I should not have a whole bone left in my body.

It was a lovely evening however, and the moon rose full and clear.   The air, delicious and balmy, was filled with the resinous scent of the pine and perfume of yellow jessamine, and we were a very jolly party, four gentlemen, with ourselves, making up our number, so I thought it good fun on the whole.   In fact, rough as the journey was, I rather enjoyed it all; it was so new a chapter in my book of travels.

Between nine and ten in the evening we arrived at a log cabin, where, until three A.M. we sat on the floor round a huge wood fire. The train then arrived and we started again, and did not stop for twenty-four hours; at least, when I say did not stop, I mean, did not leave the cars, for we really seemed to do little else but stop every few minutes. This brought us, at three A.M., to Augusta, where we were allowed to go to bed for three hours, starting again at six and travelling all day, until at seven in the evening we at last reached Savannah. Fortunately we started from the North with a large basket of provisions, that being our only luggage, the trunks having been sent by sea; and had it not been for this, I think we certainly should have starved, as we were not able to get anything to eat on the road, except at Columbia and Augusta.

The morning after our arrival in Savannah, my father came into my room to say he was off to the plantation at once, having seen some gentlemen the evening before, who told him if he wished to do anything at all in the way of planting this season, that he must not lose an hour, as it was very doubtful even now if a crop could be got in. So off he went, promising to return as soon as possible, and report what state of things he found on the island. I consoled myself by going off to church to hear Bishop Elliott, who preached one of the most beautiful sermons I ever heard, on the Resurrection, the one thought that can bring hope and comfort to these poor heart-broken people. There was hardly anyone at church out of deep mourning, and it was piteous to see so many mere girls' faces, shaded by deep crape veils and widows' caps.

I can hardly give a true idea of how crushed and sad the people are. You hear no bitterness towards the North ; they are too

sad to be bitter; their grief is overwhelming.
Nothing can make any difference to them
now; the women live in the past, and the
men only in the daily present, trying, in a
listless sort of way, to repair their ruined
fortunes. They are like so many foreigners,
whose only interest in the country is their
own individual business. Politics are never
mentioned, and they know and care less
about what is going on in Washington than
in London. They received us with open
arms, my room was filled with flowers, and
crowds of people called upon me every day,
and overwhelmed me with thanks for what I
did for their soldiers during the war, which
really did amount to but very little. I say
this, and the answer invariably is, 'Oh yes,
but your heart was with us,' which it certainly
was.

We had, before leaving the North, received two letters from Georgia, one from
an agent of the Freedmen's Bureau, and
the other from one of our neighbours, both

stating very much the same thing, which was that our former slaves had all returned to the island and were willing and ready to work for us, but refused to engage themselves to anyone else, even to their liberators, the Yankees ; but that they were very badly off, short of provisions, and would starve if something were not done for them at once, and, unless my father came directly (so wrote the agent of the Freedmen's Bureau), the negroes would be removed and made to work elsewhere.

On Wednesday, when my father returned, he reported that he had found the negroes all on the place, not only those who were there five years ago, but many who were sold three years before that. Seven had worked their way back from the up country. They received him very affectionately, and made an agreement with him to work for one half the crop, which agreement it remained to be seen if they would keep. Owing to our coming so late, only a small crop could be

planted, enough to make seed for another
year and clear expenses. I was sorry we
could do no more, but too thankful that
things were as promising as they were.
Most of the finest plantations were lying idle
for want of hands to work them, so many of
the negroes had died; 17,000 deaths were
recorded by the Freedmen's Bureau alone.
Many had been taken to the South-west, and
others preferred hanging about the towns,
making a few dollars now and then, to working regularly on the plantations; so most
people found it impossible to get any labourers, but we had as many as we wanted, and
nothing could induce our people to go anywhere else. My father also reported that
the house was bare, not a bed nor chair left,
and that he had been sleeping on the floor,
with a piece of wood for a pillow and a few
negro blankets for his covering. This I
could hardly do, and as he could attend to
nothing but the planting, we agreed that he
should devote himself to that, while I looked

after some furniture. So the day after, armed with five hundred bushels of seed rice, corn, bacon, a straw mattress, and a tub, he started off again for the plantation, leaving me to buy tables and chairs, pots and pans.

We heard that our overseer had removed many of the things to the interior with the negroes for safety on the approach of the Yankees, so I wrote to him about them, waiting to know what he had saved of our old furniture, before buying anything new. This done, I decided to proceed with my household goods to the plantation, arrange things as comfortably as possible, and then return to the North.

I cannot give a better idea of the condition of things I found on the Island than by copying the following letter written at the time.

April 12, 1866.

Dearest S——, I have relapsed into barbarism total! How I do wish you could see me ; you would be so disgusted. Well, I

know now what the necessaries of life mean,
and am surprised to find how few they are,
and how many things we consider absolutely
necessary which are really luxuries.

When I wrote last I was waiting in
Savannah for the arrival of some things the
overseer had taken from the Island, which I
wished to look over before I made any
further purchases for the house. When they
came, however, they looked more like the
possessions of an Irish emigrant than anything else ; the house linen fortunately was
in pretty good order, but the rest I fancy had
furnished the overseer's house in the country
ever since the war ; the silver never reappeared. So I began my purchases with
twelve common wooden chairs, four wash-
stands, four bedsteads, four large tubs, two
bureaux, two large tables and four smaller
ones, some china, and one common lounge,
my one luxury—and this finished the list.

Thus supplied, my maid and I started
last Saturday morning for the Island ; half-

way down we stuck fast on a sand-bar in the
river, where we remained six hours, very hot,
and devoured by sand-flies, till the tide came
in again and floated us off, which pleasant little
episode brought us to Darien at 1 A.M. My
father was there, however, to meet us with
our own boat, and as it was bright moonlight
we got off with all our things, and were
rowed across to the island by four of our old
negroes.

I wish I could give you any idea of the
house. The floors were bare, of course, many
of the panes were out of the windows, and the
plaster in many places was off the walls,
while one table and two old chairs constituted
the furniture. It was pretty desolate, and
my father looked at me in some anxiety to
see how it would affect me, and seemed
greatly relieved when I burst out laughing.
My bed was soon unpacked and made, my
tub filled, my basin and pitcher mounted on
a barrel, and I settled for the rest of the
night.

The next morning I and my little German maid, who fortunately takes everything very cheerily, went to work, and together we made things quite comfortable ; unpacked our tables and chairs, put up some curtains (made out of some white muslin I had brought down for petticoats) edged with pink calico, covered the tables with two bright-coloured covers I found in the trunk of house linen, had the windows mended, hung up my picture of General Lee (which had been sent to me the day before I left Philadelphia) over the mantelpiece, and put my writing things and nicknacks on the table, so that when my father and Mr. J—— came in they looked round in perfect astonishment, and quite rewarded me by their praise.

Our kitchen arrangements would amuse you. I have one large pot, one frying-pan, one tin saucepan, and this is all ; and yet you would be astonished to see how much our cook accomplishes with these three utensils, and the things don't taste *very* much alike.

Yesterday one of the negroes shot and gave me a magnificent wild turkey, which we roasted on one stick set up between two others before the fire, and capital it was. The broiling is done on two old pieces of iron laid over the ashes. Our food consists of corn and rice bread, rice, and fish caught fresh every morning out of the river, oysters, turtle soup, and occasionally a wild turkey or duck. Other meat, as yet, it is impossible to get.

Is it not all strange and funny? I feel like Robinson Crusoe with three hundred men Fridays. Then my desert really blooms like the rose. On the acre of ground enclosed about the house are a superb magnolia tree, covered with its queenly flowers, roses running wild in every direction; orange, fig, and peach trees now in blossom, give promise of fruit later on, while every tree and bush is alive with red-birds, mocking-birds, black-birds, and jays, so as I sit on the piazza the air comes to me laden with sweet smells and sweet sounds of all descriptions.

There are some drawbacks; fleas, sand-
flies, and mosquitoes remind us that we are not
quite in Heaven, and I agree with my laundry
woman, Phillis, who upon my maid's remon-
strating with her for taking all day to wash a
few towels, replied, ' Dat's true, Miss Louisa,
but de fleas jist have no principle, and dey
bites me so all de time, I jist have to stop
to scratch.'

The negroes seem perfectly happy at
getting back to the old place and having us
there, and I have been deeply touched by
many instances of devotion on their part.
On Sunday morning, after their church,
having nothing to do, they all came to see
me, and I must have shaken hands with
nearly four hundred. They were full of their
troubles and sufferings up the country during
the war, and the invariable winding up was,
'Tank the Lord, missus, we's back, and sees
you and massa again.' I said to about twenty
strong men, ' Well, you know you are free and
your own masters now,' when they broke out

with, ' No, missus, we belong to you ; we be
yours as long as we lib.'

Nearly all who have lived through the
terrible suffering of these past four years
have come back, as well as many of those
who were sold seven years ago. Their good
character was so well known throughout the
State that people were very anxious to hire
them and induce them to remain in the ' up
country,' and told them all sorts of stories to
keep them, among others that my father
was dead, but all in vain. One old man said,
' If massa be dead den, I'll go back to the old
place and mourn for him.' So they not only
refused good wages, but in many cases spent
all they had to get back, a fact that speaks
louder than words as to their feeling for their
old master and former treatment.

Our overseer, who was responsible for all
our property, has little or nothing to give us
back, while everything that was left in charge
of the negroes has been taken care of and
given back to us without the hope or wish of

reward. One old man has guarded the stock so well from both Southern and Northern marauders, that he has now ninety odd sheep and thirty cows under his care. Unfortunately they are on a pine tract some twelve miles away up the river, and as we have no means of transporting them we cannot get them until next year.

One old couple came up yesterday from St. Simon's, Uncle John and Mum Peggy, with five dollars in silver half-dollars tied up in a bag, which they said a Yankee captain had given them the second year of the war for some chickens, and this money these two old people had kept through all their want and suffering for three years because it had been paid for fowls belonging to us. I wonder whether white servants would be so faithful or honest! My father was much moved at this act of faithfulness, and intends to have something made out of the silver to commemorate the event, having returned them the same amount in other money.

One of the great difficulties of this new state of things is, what is to be done with the old people who are too old, and the children who are too young, to work ?   One Northern General said to a planter, in answer to this question, 'Well, I suppose they must die,' which, indeed, seems the only thing for them to do.   To-day Mr. J—— tells me my father has agreed to support the children for three years, and the old people till they die, that is, feed and clothe them.   Fortunately, as we have some property at the North we are able to do this, but most of the planters are utterly ruined and have no money to buy food for their own families, so on their plantations I do not see what else is to become of the negroes who cannot work except to die.

Yours affectionately,

F.——.

The prospect of getting in the crop did not grow more promising as time went on. The negroes talked a great deal about their desire and intention to work for us, but their idea of work, unaided by the stern law of necessity, is very vague, some of them working only half a day and some even less. I don't think one does a really honest full day's work, and so of course not half the necessary amount is done and I am afraid never will be again, and so our properties will soon be utterly worthless, for no crop can be raised by such labour as this, and no negro will work if he can help it, and is quite satisfied just to scrape along doing an odd job here and there to earn money enough to buy a little food.[1] They are affectionate and often trustworthy and honest, but so hopelessly lazy as to be almost worthless as labourers.

My father was quite encouraged at first, the people seemed so willing to work and said so much about their intention of doing so ; but not many days after they started he came in quite disheartened, saying that half

[1] N.B. I was mistaken. In the years 1877 and 1880 upwards of thirty thousand bushels of rice was raised on the place by these same negroes.

the hands had left the fields at one o'clock and the rest by three o'clock, and this just at our busiest time. Half a day's work will keep them from starving, but won't raise a crop. Our contract with them is for half the crop ; that is, one half to be divided among them, according to each man's rate of work, we letting them have in the meantime necessary food, clothing, and money for their present wants (as they have not a penny) which is to be deducted from whatever is due to them at the end of the year.

This we found the best arrangement to make with them, for if we paid them wages, the first five dollars they made would have seemed like so large a sum to them, that they would have imagined their fortunes made and refused to work any more. But even this arrangement had its objections, for they told us, when they missed working two or three days a week, that they were losers by it as well as ourselves, half the crop being theirs. But they could not see that this sort of work would not raise any crop at all, and that such should be the result was quite beyond their comprehension. They were quite convinced that if six days' work would raise a whole crop, three days' work would raise half a one, with which they as partners were satisfied, and so it seemed as if we should have to be too.

The rice plantation becoming unhealthy early in May, we removed to St. Simon's, a sea island on the coast, about fifteen miles from Butler's Island, where the famous Sea Island cotton had formerly been raised. This place had been twice in possession of the Northern troops during the war, and the negroes had consequently been brought under the influence of Northerners, some of whom had filled the poor people's minds with all sorts of vain hopes and ideas, among others that their former masters would not be allowed to return, and the land was theirs, a thing many of them believed, and they had planted both corn and cotton to a considerable extent. To disabuse their minds of this notion my father determined to put in a few acres of cotton, although the lateness of the season and work at Butler's Island prevented planting of any extent being done this season.

Our departure from one place and arrival at another was very characteristic. The house on St. Simon's being entirely stripped of furniture, we had to take our scanty provision of household goods down with us from Butler's Island by raft, our only means of transportation. Having learned from the negroes that the tide turned at six A.M., and to reach St. Simon's that day it would be necessary to start on the first of the ebb, we went to bed the night before, all agreeing to get up at four the next morning, so as to have our beds &c. on board and ready to start by six. By five, Mr. J——, my maid, and I were ready and our things on board, but nothing would induce my father to get up until eight o'clock, when he appeared on the wharf in his dressing-gown, clapped his hands to his head, exclaiming, ' My gracious ! that flat should be off; just look at the tide,' which indeed had then been running down two good hours. Without a word I had his bedroom furniture put on, and ordered the men to push off, which they did just as my father reappeared, calling out that half his things had been left behind, a remark which was fortunately useless as far as the flat was concerned, as it was rapidly disappearing on the swift current down the river.

At three o'clock we started in a large six-oared boat, with all the things forgotten in the morning piled in. The day was cloudless, the air soft and balmy ; the wild semi-tropical vegetation that edged the river on both sides beautiful beyond description ; the tender new spring green of the deciduous trees and shrubs, mingling with the dark green of the evergreen cypress, magnolia, and bay, all wreathed and bound together with the yellow jessamine and fringed with the soft delicate grey moss which floated from every branch and twig. Not a sound broke the stillness but the dip of our oars in the water, accompanied by the wild minor chant of the negro boat-men, who sang nearly the whole way down, keeping time with the stroke of the oar.

Half-way down we passed the unfortunate raft stuck in the mud, caught by the turning tide. Unable to help it, we left it to wait the return of the ebb, not however without painful reflections, as we had had no dinner before starting, and our cook with his frying-pan and saucepan, was perched on a bag of rice on the raft.

Shortly after five o'clock we reached St. Simon's, and found the house a fair-sized comfortable building, with a wide piazza running all round it, but without so much as a stool or bench in it. So, hungry and tired, we sat down on the floor, to await the arrival of the things. Night came on, but we had no candles, and so sat on in darkness till after ten o'clock, when the raft arrived with almost everything soaked through, the result of a heavy thunder shower which had come on while it was stuck fast. This I confess was more than I could bear, and I burst out crying. A little cold meat and some bread consoled me somewhat, and finding the blankets had fortunately escaped the wetting, we spread these on the floor over the wet mattresses, and, all dressed, slowly and sadly laid us down to sleep.

The next morning the sun was shining as it only can shine in a southern sky, and the birds were singing as they only can sing in such sunlight. The soft sea air blew in at the window, mingled with the aromatic fragrance of the pines, and I forgot all my miseries, and was enchanted and happy. After breakfast, which was a repetition of last night's supper, with the addition of milk-less tea, I set about seeing how the house could be made comfortable. There were four good-sized rooms down and two upstairs, with a hall ten feet wide running through the

house, and a wide verandah shut in from the
sun by Venetian shades running round it;
the kitchen, with the servants' quarters, was
as usual detached. A nice enough house,
capable of being made both pretty and comfortable, which in time I hope to do.

My father spent the time in talking to the
negroes, of whom there were about fifty on
the place, making arrangements with them
for work, more to establish his right to the
place than from any real good we expect to
do this year. We found them in a very
different frame of mind from the negroes on
Butler's Island, who having been removed
the first year of the war, had never been
brought into contact with either army, and
remained the same demonstrative and noisy
childish people they had always been. The
negroes on St. Simon's had always been the
most intelligent, having belonged to an older
estate, and a picked lot, but besides, they
had tasted of the tree of knowledge. They
were perfectly respectful, but quiet, and

evidently disappointed to find they were not the masters of the soil and that their new friends the Yankees had deceived them. Many of them had planted a considerable quantity of corn and cotton, and this my father told them they might have, but that they must put in twenty acres for him, for which he would give them food and clothing, and another year, when he hoped to put in several hundred acres, they should share the crop. They consented without any show of either pleasure or the reverse, and went to work almost immediately under the old negro foreman or driver, who had managed the place before the war.

They still showed that they had confidence in my father, for when a miserable creature, an agent of the Freedmen's Bureau, who was our ruler then, and regulated all our contracts with our negroes, told them that they would be fools to believe that my father would really let them have all the crops they had planted before he came, and they would see that he would claim at least half, they replied, 'No, sir, our master is a just man ; he has never lied to us, and we believe him.' Rather taken aback by this, he turned to an old driver who was the principal person present, and said, 'Why, Bram, how can you care so much for your master—he sold you a few years ago ?' 'Yes, sir,' replied the old man, 'he sold me and I was very unhappy, but he came to me and said, " Bram, I am in great trouble ; I have no money and I have to sell some of the people, but I know where you are all going to, and will buy you back again as soon as I can." And, sir, he told me, Juba, my old wife, must go with me, for though she was not strong, and the gentleman who bought me would not buy her, master said he could not let man and wife be separated ; and so, sir, I said, " Master, if you will keep me I will work for you as long as I live, but if you in trouble and it help you to sell me, sell me, master, I am willing." And now that we free, I come back to my old home and my old master, and stay here till I die." ' This story the agent told a Northern friend of ours in utter astonishment.

To show what perfect confidence my father had on his side in his old slaves, the day after starting the work here, he returned to Butler's Island, leaving me and my maid entirely alone, with no white person within eight miles of us, and in a house on no door of which was there more than a latch, and neither then nor afterwards, when I was alone on the plantation with the negroes for weeks at a time, had I the slightest feeling of fear, except one night, when I had a fright which made me quite ill for two days, although it turned out to be a most absurd cause of terror. The quiet and solitude of the plantation was absolute, and at night there was not a movement, the negro settlement being two miles away from the house.

I was awaked one night about two o'clock by a noise at the river landing, which was not the eighth of a mile from the house, and on listening, heard talking, shouting, and apparently struggling. I got up and called my little German maid, who after listening a moment said, ' It is a fight, and I think the men are drunk.' Knowing that it could not be our own men, I made up my mind that a party of strange and drunken negroes were trying to land, and that my people were trying to prevent them. Knowing how few my people were, I felt for one moment utterly terrified and helpless, as indeed I was. Then I took two small pistols my father had left with me, and putting them full cock, and followed by my maid, who I must say was wonderfully brave, I proceeded out of the house to the nearest hut, where my man servant lived. I was a little reassured to hear his voice in answer when I called, and I sent him down to the river to see what was the matter. It turned out to be a raft full of mules from Butler's Island, which I had not expected, and who objected to being landed, hence the struggling and shouting. I had been too terrified to laugh, and suddenly becoming aware of the two pistols at full cock in my hands, was then seized with my natural terror of firearms. So I laid them, full cocked as they were, in a drawer, where they remained for several days, until my father came and uncocked them. This was my only real fright, although for the next two or three years we were constantly hearing wild rumours of intended negro insurrections, which however, as I never quite believed, did not frighten me.

I had a pretty hard time of it that first year, owing to my wretched servants, and to the scarcity of provisions of all sorts. The country was absolutely swept ; not a chicken, not an egg was left, and for weeks I lived on hominy, rice, and fish, with an occasional bit of venison. The negroes said the Yankees had eaten up everything, and one old woman told me they had refused to pay her for the eggs, but after they had eaten them said

they were addled; but I think the people
generally had not much to complain of.
The only two good servants we had remained with my father at Butler's Island,
and mine were all raw field hands, to whom
everything was new and strange, and who
were really savages.   My white maid, watch-
ing my sable housemaid one morning
through the door, saw her dip my tooth-
brush in the tub in which I had just bathed,
and with my small hand-glass in the other
hand, in which she was attentively regarding
the operation, proceed to scrub her teeth
with the brush.   It is needless to say I presented her with that one, and locked my new
one up as soon as I had finished using it.

My cook made all the flour and sugar I
gave him (my own allowance of which was
very small) into sweet cakes, most of which
he ate himself, and when I scolded him,
cried.   The young man who was with us,
dying of consumption, was my chief anxiety,
for he was terribly ill, and could not eat the

fare I did, and to get anything else was an impossibility. I scoured the island one day in search of chickens, but only succeeded in getting one old cock, of which my wretched cook made such a mess that Mr. J—— could not touch it after it was done. I tried my own hand at cooking, but without much success, not knowing really how to cook a potato, besides which the roof of the kitchen leaked badly, and as we had frequent showers, I often had to cook, holding up an umbrella in one hand and stirring with the other.

I remained on St. Simon's Island until the end of July, my father coming down from Butler's Island from Saturday till Monday every week for rest, which he sorely needed, for although he had got the negroes into something like working order, they required constant personal supervision, which on the rice fields in midsummer was frightfully trying, particularly as, after the day's work was over, he had to row a mile across

the river, and then drive out six miles to the
hut in the pine woods where he slept.   The
salt air, quiet, and peace of St. Simon's was
therefore a delightful rest and change, and
he refused to give an order when he came
down, referring all the negroes to me.   One
man whom he had put off in this way
several times, revenged himself one day
when my father told him to get a mule cart
ready, by saying, ' Does missus say so ? '
which, however, was more fun than impu-
dence.

I will finish my account of this year by
copying a letter written on the spot at the
time.

Hampton Point : July 9, 1866.

Dearest S——, I did not expect to write
to you again from my desert island.   Aber ich
bin als noch hier, rapidly approaching the
pulpy gelatinous state.   Three times have I
settled upon a day for leaving, and three
times have I put it off ; the truth is, I am
very busy, very useful, and very happy.

Then I am anxious about leaving my father, for fear the unusual exposure to this Southern sun may make him ill ; and with no doctor, no nurse, no medicine, and no proper food nearer than Savannah, it would be a serious thing to be ill here.

I am just learning to be an experienced cook and doctress, for the negroes come to me with every sort of complaint to be treated, and I prescribe for all, pills and poultices being my favourite remedies. I was rather nervous about it at first, but have grown bolder since I find what good results always follow my doses. Faith certainly has a great deal to do with it, and that is unbounded on the part of my patients, who would swallow a red-hot poker if I ordered it.

The other day an old woman of over eighty came for a dose, so I prescribed a small one of castor oil, which pleased her so much she returned the next day to have it repeated, and again a third time, on which I remonstrated and said, ' No, Mum Charlotte,

you are too old to be dosing yourself so.' To
which she replied, 'Den, dear missus, do
give me some for put on outside, for ain't
you me mudder ? '

We are living directly on the Point, in the
house formerly occupied by the overseer, a
much pleasanter and prettier situation, I think,
than the Hill House, in which you lived when
you were here. Of course it is all very rough
and overgrown now, but with the pretty water
view across which you look to the wide
stretch of broad green salt marsh, which at
sunset turns the most wonderful gold bronze
colour, and the magnolia, orange, and superb
live oak trees around and near the house,
it might, by a little judicious clearing and
pruning, be made quite lovely, and if I am
here next winter, as I suppose I shall be,
I shall try my hand at a little landscape-
gardening.

The fishing is grand, and we have fresh
fish for breakfast, dinner, and tea. Our fisherman, one of our old slaves, is a great character,

and quite as enthusiastic about fishing as I am. I have been out once or twice with him, but not for deep-sea fishing yet, which however I hope to do soon, as he brings in the most magnificent bass, and blue fish weighing twenty and thirty pounds. The other day when we were out it began to thunder, and he said, ' Dere missus, go home. No use to fish more. De fish mind de voice of de Lord better dan we poor mortals, and when it tunders dey go right down to de bottom of de sea.'

I have two little pet bears, the funniest, jolliest little beasts imaginable. They have no teeth, being only six weeks old, and have to be fed on milk, which they will drink out of a dish if I hold it very quietly, but if I make the least noise they rush off, get up on their hind legs, and hiss and spit at me like cats. One spends his time turning summersets, and the other lies flat on his back, with his two little paws over his nose. They are too delightful.

I have been very fortunate in my weather, for although the days are terribly hot, there is always a pleasant sea-breeze, and the evenings and nights are delightfully cool. In fact I have suffered much less from the heat here than I usually do near Philadelphia in summer. The great trouble is that I cannot walk at all on account of the snakes, of which I live in terror. The daytime is too hot for them, and they take their walks abroad in the cool of the eveniug.

Last evening I was sauntering up the road, when about a quarter of a mile from the house I saw something moving very slowly across the path. At first I thought it was a cat, crouching as they do just before they spring, but in a moment more I saw it was a huge rattlesnake, as large round as my arm and quite six feet long. Two little birds were hovering over him, fluttering lower and lower every moment, fascinated by his evil eye and forked tongue which kept dart-ing in and out. He was much too busy to notice me, so after looking at him for one moment I flew back to the house, shrieking with all my might, ' Pierce ! John ! Alex ! William !' Hearing my voice they all rushed out, and, armed with sticks, axes, and spades, we proceeded to look for the monster, who however had crawled into the thick bushes when we had reached the spot, and although we could hear him rattle violently when we struck the bushes, the negroes could not see him, and were afraid to go into the thick undergrowth after him, so he still lives to walk abroad, and I—to stay at home.

Mr. James Hamilton Cooper died last week, and was buried at the little church on the island here yesterday. The whole thing was sad in the extreme, and a fit illustration of this people and country. Three years ago he was smitten with paralysis, the result of grief at the loss of his son, loss of his property, and the ruin of all his hopes and prospects ; since which his life has been one of great suffering, until a few days ago, when death released him. Hearing from his son of his death, and the time fixed for his funeral, my father and I drove down in the old mule cart, our only conveyance, nine miles to the church. Here a most terrible scene of desolation met us. The steps of the church were broken down, so we had to walk up a plank to get in ; the roof was fallen in, so that the sun streamed down on our heads ; while the seats were all cut up and marked with the names of Northern soldiers, who had been quartered there during the war. The graveyard was so overgrown with weeds and bushes, and tangled with cob-web like grey moss, that we had difficulty in making our way through to the freshly dug grave.

In about half an hour the funeral party arrived. The coffin was in a cart drawn by one miserable horse, and was followed by the Cooper family on foot, having come this way from the landing, two miles off. From the cart to the grave the coffin was carried by four old family negroes, faithful to the end. Standing there I said to myself, 'Some day justice will be done, and the Truth shall be heard above the political din of slander and lies, and the Northern people shall see things as they are, and not through the dark veil of envy, hatred, and malice.' Good-bye. I sail on the 21st for the North.

Yours affectionately,

F——

CHAPTER II.

A FRESH START.

My return to the South in 1867 was much
later than I had expected it would be when
I left the previous summer, but my father
was repairing the house on Butler's Island,
and put off my coming, hoping to have things
more comfortable for me. When, however,
March came, and it was still unfinished, I
determined to wait no longer, but if necessary
to go direct to St. Simon's, and not to Butler's
Island at all. Wishing to make our habitation
more comfortable than it was last year, I
took from the North six large boxes, contain-
ing carpets, curtains, books, and various household articles, and accompanied by my maid, a
negro lad I had taken up with me, named

Pierce, and a little girl of ten, whom I was taking South for companionship, I started again for Georgia on March 10.

Owing to a mistake about my ticket I took the wrong route, went two hundred miles out of my way, and found myself one night, or rather morning at 2 A.M., landed in Augusta, where I was forced to remain until six the next morning, and where I had never been before and did not know anyone even by name. I felt rather nervous, but picking out the most respectable-looking man among my fellow-travellers, I asked him to recommend me to the best hotel in Augusta, which he did, and on my arriving at it found to my great joy that it was kept by Mr. Nickleson, formerly of the Mills House, Charleston, who knew who I was perfectly, received me most courteously, and after giving me first a comfortable bed, and then a good breakfast, sent me off the following morning with a nice little luncheon put up, a most necessary consideration, for it was impossible to get anything to

eat on the road, and the day before we had
nothing but some biscuits and an orange
which we happened to have brought with us.
We reached Savannah that evening, having
been exactly ninety-four hours on the road,
with no longer rest than the one at Augusta
of four hours.

In Savannah I remained a week, and the
following Saturday started for St. Simon's
Island, sticking fast in the mud as usual, and
being delayed in consequence six hours.   The
K——'s were on board with us, returning to
their home for the first time since the war,
bringing with them all their household goods
and chattels; and a funnier sight than our
disembarkation was never seen, as we looked
like a genuine party of emigrants.   The little
wharf was covered with beds, tables, chairs,
ploughs, pots, pans, boxes, and trunks, for we
also had quantities of things of all kinds.   A
mule cart awaited us and an ox cart them,
into which elegant conveyance we clambered,
surrounded by our beds and pots and pans,

and solemnly took our departure, each in a
separate direction, for the opposite ends of the
island.

I had not gone far when I met Major
D——, a young Philadelphian, who with his
brother had rented a plantation next ours, and
who is the proud possessor of a horse and
waggon, in which he kindly offered to drive
me to Hampton Point, an offer I very gladly
accepted, thereby reaching my destination
sooner than I should otherwise have done.
I thought things would be better this year,
but notwithstanding my Northern luxuries, I
found it much harder to get along. My
father, finding it impossible to manage the rice
plantation on Butler's Island and the cotton
one here, gladly agreed to the Misses D——'s
offer to plant on shares, they undertaking the
management here, which allowed him to devote all his time to the other place. The
consequence is that 'the crop,' being the only
thing thought of, every able-bodied man,
woman, and child is engaged on it, and I find

my household staff reduced to two. I inquired after my friend Fisherman George,
'oh, he was ploughing,' so I could have no fish,
my cook and his wife have departed altogether, and my washerwoman and semp-
stress 'are picking cotton seed,' so Major
D—— smilingly informed me, leaving me
Daphne, who is expecting her eleventh confinement in less than a month, and Alex her
husband, who invariably is taken ill just as he
ought to get dinner, and Pierce, who since his
winter at the North is too fine to do anything
but wait at table. So I cook, and my maid
does the housework, and as it has rained hard
for three days and the kitchen roof is half off,
I cook in the dining-room or parlour. Fortunately, my provisions are so limited that I have
not much to cook ; for five days my food has
consisted of hard pilot biscuits, grits cooked
in different ways, oysters, and twice, as a great
treat, ham and eggs. I brought a box of
preserves from the North with me, but half
of them upset, and the rest were spoilt.

One window is entirely without a sash, so I have to keep the shutters closed all the time, and over the other I have pasted three pieces of paper where panes should be. My bed stood under a hole in the roof, through which the rain came, and I think if it rains much more there will not be a dry spot left in the house. However, as I would not wait at the North till the house on Butler's Island was finished, I have no one to blame for my present sufferings but myself, and when I get some servants and food from there, I shall be better off.

The people seem to me working fairly well, but Major D——, used only to Northern labour, is in despair, and says they don't do more than half a day's work, and that he has often to go from house to house to drive them out to work, and then has to sit under a tree in the field to see they don't run away.

A Mr. G—— from New York has bought Canon's Point, and is going to the greatest

expense to stock it with mules and farming
implements of all sorts, insisting upon it that
we Southerners don't know how to manage
our own places or negroes, and he will show
us, but I think he will find out his mistake.[1]
My father reported the negroes on Butler's

[1] The history of Canon's Point is as follows. Mr. G——
having started by putting the negroes on regular wages
expecting them to do regular work in return, and not being
at all prepared to go through the lengthy conversations and
explanations which they required, utterly failed in his attempts
either to manage the negroes or to get any work out of them.
Some ran off, some turned sulky, and some stayed and did
about half the work.   So that at the end of two years he gave
the place up in perfect disgust, a little to our amusement, as
he had been so sure, like many another Northern man, that
all the negroes wanted was regular work and regular wages,
overlooking entirely the character of the people he was
dealing with, who required a different treatment every day
almost ; sometimes coaxing, sometimes scolding, sometimes
punishing, sometimes indulging, and always—unlimited
patience.   After Mr. G—— failed in his management of the
negroes he gave the place up, leaving an agent there merely
to keep possession of the property.   This man in turn moved
off, leaving about fifty negro families in undisputed possession, who two years later were driven off by a new tenant
who undertook to charge them high rent for their land ; and
it is now finally in the hands of a Western farmer and his
son, who told my husband last winter that they were delighted
with the place and climate, but had not learned to manage
the negroes yet, as when he scolded them they got scared
and ran off, and when he did not they would not work.

Island as working very well, although requiring constant supervision. That they should
be working well is a favourable sign of their
improved steadiness, for, as last year's crop
is not yet sold, no division has been possible.
So they have begun a second year, not having yet been paid for the first, and meanwhile
they are allowed to draw what food, clothing,
and money they want, all of which I fear
will make trouble when the day of settlement
comes, but it is pleasant to see how completely
they trust us.

On both places the work is done on the
old system, by task. We tried working by the
day, indeed I think we were obliged to do so
by the agent of the Freedmen's Bureau, to
whom all our contracts had to be submitted,
but we found it did not answer at all, the
negroes themselves begging to be allowed to
go back to the old task system. One man
indignantly asked Major D—— what the use
of being free was, if he had to work harder
than when he was a slave. To which Major

D——, exasperated by their laziness, replied that they would find being free meant harder work than they had ever done before, or starvation.

In all other ways the work went on just as it did in the old times. The force, of about three hundred, was divided into gangs, each working under a head man—the old negro drivers, who are now called captains, out of compliment to the changed times. These men make a return of the work each night, and it is very amusing to hear them say, as each man's name is called, ' He done him work ; ' ' He done half him task ;' or 'Ain't sh'um' (have not seen him). They often did overwork when urged, and were of course credited for the same on the books. To make them do odd jobs was hopeless, as I found when I got some hands from Butler's Island, and tried to make them clear up the grounds about the house, cut the undergrowth and make a garden, &c. Unless I stayed on the spot all the time, the instant I disappeared they disappeared as well. On one occasion, having succeeded in getting a couple of cows, I set a man to churn some butter. After leaving him for a few moments, I returned to find him sitting on the floor with the churn between his legs, turning the handle slowly, about once a minute. 'Cato,' I exclaimed, 'that will never do. You must turn just as fast as ever you can to make butter!' Looking up very gravely, he replied, 'Missus, in dis country de butter must be coaxed; der no good to hurry.' And I generally found that if I wanted a thing done I first had to tell the negroes to do it, then show them how, and finally do it myself. Their way of managing not to do it was very ingenious, for they always were perfectly good-tempered, and received my orders with, 'Dat's so, missus; just as missus says,' and then always somehow or other left the thing undone.

The old people were up to all sorts of tricks to impose upon my charity, and get some favour out of me. They were far too old

and infirm to work for me, but once let them
get a bit of ground of their own given to them,
and they became quite young and strong
again. One old woman, called Charity, who
represented herself as unable to move, and
entirely dependent on my goodness for food
&c., I found was in the habit of walking
six miles almost every day to take eggs to
Major D—— to sell. I was complaining
once to him of my want of provisions, and
said, 'I can't even get eggs ; in old times all the
old women had eggs and chickens to sell, but
they none of them seem to have any left.'
'Why,' said he, 'we get eggs regularly from
one of your old women, who walks down
every day or two to us ; Charity her name is.'
'Charity! impossible,' I exclaimed ; 'she can
hardly crawl round here from her hut.' 'It is
true though, nevertheless,' said he. So the
next time Mistress Charity presented herself,
almost on all fours, and said, 'Do, dear
missus, give me something for eat,' I said,
'No, you old humbug, I won't give you one

thing more. You know how much I want eggs, and yet you never told me you had any, and take them off to Major D——— to sell, because you think if I know you have eggs to sell I won't give you things.' For one moment the old wretch was taken aback at being found out, and then her ready negro wit came to her aid, and she exclaimed with a horrified and indignant air, 'Me sell eggs to me dear missus. Neber *sell* her eggs ; gib dem to her.' I need hardly say she had never given me one, but after that did sell them to me.

I spent my birthday at the South, and my maid telling the people that it was my birthday, they came up in the evening to 'shout for me.' A negro must dance and sing, and as their religion, which is very strict in such matters, forbids secular dancing, they take it out in religious exercise, call it 'shouting,' and explained to me that the difference between the two was, that in their religious dancing they did not 'lift the heel.' All day they were bringing me little presents of honey, eggs, flowers, &c., and in the evening about fifty of them, of all sizes and ages and of both sexes, headed by old Uncle John, the preacher, collected in front of the house to 'shout.' First they lit two huge fires of blazing pine logs, around which they began to move with a slow shuffling step, singing a hymn beginning ' I wants to climb up Jacob's ladder.' Getting warmed up by degrees, they went faster and faster, shouting louder and louder, until they looked like a parcel of mad fiends. The children, finding themselves kicked over in the general *mêlée*, formed a circle on their own account, and went round like small catherine wheels.

When, after nearly an hour's performance, I went down to thank them, and to stop them —for it was getting dreadful, and I thought some of them would have fits—I found it no easy matter to do so, they were so excited. One of them, rushing up to my father, seized him by the hand, exclaiming, ' Massa, when

your birthday? We must "shout" for you.'
'Oh, Tony,' said my father, 'my birthday is
long passed.' Upon which the excited Tony
turned to Major D——, who with Mr. G——
had been dining with us, and said, 'Well den,
Massa Charlie, when yours?' I told him finally
it was Miss Sarah's birthday as well as mine.
On hearing this he turned to the people, saying, 'Children, hear de'y (hear do you), dis
Miss Sarah's birthday too. You must shout
so loud Miss Sarah hear you all de way to de
North!' At which off they went again, harder
than ever. Dear old Uncle John came up to
me, and taking my hands in his, said, 'God
bless you, missus, my dear missus.' My father,
who was standing near, put his arm round
the old man's shoulders, and said, 'You have
seen five generations of us now, John, haven't
you?' 'Yes, massa,' said John, 'Miss Sarah's
little boy be de fifth; bless de Lord.' Both
Major D—— and Mr. G—— spoke of this
afterwards, saying 'How fond your father is of
the people.' 'Yes,' said I, 'this is a relation-

ship you Northern people can't understand, and will soon destroy.'

I remained on St. Simon's Island this summer until the end of July, enjoying every moment of my time. The climate was perfect, and I had a delightful Southern-bred mare, on which I used to take long rides every day. My father had seen her running about the streets of Darien, and thought her so hand-some he had bought her from the man who professed to own her. She was afterwards claimed by a gentleman from Virginia, who said she was a sister of Planet's, and had been raised on his brother's plantation. When the war ended he had gone to Texas, leaving her with a friend out of whose stable she had been stolen by a deserter from the 12th Maine Regiment, who sold her to the man from whom my father bought her. The story, which was proved to be quite ˙true, nearly cost me my mare, who was the dearest and most intelligent horse I ever had, and who grew to know me so well that she would follow me about like a dog, and come from the furthest end of her pasture when she heard my voice, but fortunately the owner at last agreed to a compromise, and I kept my beauty.

Twice a week I rode nine miles to Frederika, our post town, to get and take our letters, and often, with a little bundle of clothes strapped on behind my saddle, I rode down twelve miles to the south end of the island, and spent the night with my dear friends the K——'s, returning the next morning before the heat of the day. There was a good shell road the whole twelve miles, and six of it at least ran through a beautiful wood of pines and live oak, with an undergrowth of the picturesque dwarf palmetto and sweet-smelling bay. In many places the trees met overhead, through which the sun broke in showers of gold, lighting up the red trunks of the pines and soft green underneath, while the grey moss floated silently overhead like a gossamer veil, covering the whole. I never met a human being, nor heard a sound save the notes of the different birds, and the soft murmur of the wind through the tall pines, which came to me laden with their fragrant aroma, mingled with the sweet salt breeze from the sea.

I have often thought since, that it was really hardly safe for me to ride about alone, or indeed live alone, as I did half the week; but I believe there was less danger in doing so then, than there would be now. The serpent had not entered into my paradise.

One day I went on a deer hunt with some of the gentlemen, quite as much in hopes of getting some venison as of seeing any real sport. My diet of ham, eggs, fish, rice, hominy, to which latterly, endless watermelons had been added, had become almost intolerable to me, and I absolutely longed for animal food. The morning was perfect and I was very much excited, although I did not see any deer. They shot one, however, and generously gave me half. We were to have gone again, but the weather got warm and the rattlesnakes came out, so it was not safe.

My neighbours the H——'s were great sportsmen, and had before the war a famous pack of hounds, of which a story is told that, after chasing a deer all one day and across two rivers, the gentlemen returned home worn out, and without either deer or hounds. After waiting for two weeks for the return of the dogs, they went out to look for them, and on a neighbouring island found the skeletons of their hounds, in a circle round the skeleton of a deer. Fortunately, one or two of this breed had been left behind, and they were still hunting with them, and after our first hunt often sent me presents of venison, which were most acceptable.

But while my summer was gliding away in such peace and happiness, things outside were growing more and more disturbed, and my father from time to time brought me news of political disturbances, and a general growing restlessness among the negroes, which he feared would end in great trouble and destroy their usefulness as labourers. Our properties in such a case would have become worthless. White labour could be used on these sea islands, but never on the rice fields, which if we lost our negro labourers would have to be abandoned. A letter written at that time shows how different reports reached and affected us then, and also the condition our part of the South was in, the truth of which never has been known.

St. Simon's Island : June 23, 1867.

Dearest S——, We are, I am afraid, going to have terrible trouble by-and-by with the negroes, and I see nothing but gloomy prospects for us ahead. The unlimited power that the war has put into the hands of the present Government at Washington seems to have turned the heads of the party now in office, and they don't know where to stop. The whole South is settled and quiet, and the people too ruined and crushed to do any-thing against the Government, even if they felt so inclined, and all are returning to their former peaceful pursuits, trying to rebuild their fortunes, and thinking of nothing else. Yet the treatment we receive from the Government becomes more and more severe every day, the last act being to divide the whole South into five military districts, putting each under the command of a United States General, doing away with all civil courts and law. Even D——, who you know is a Northern republican, says it is most unjustifiable, not being in any way authorised by the existing state of things, which he confesses he finds very different from what he expected before he came. If they would frankly say they intend to keep us down, it would be fairer than making a pretence of readmitting us to equal rights, and then trumping up stories of violence to give a show of justice to treating us as the conquered foes of the most despotic Government on earth, and by exciting the negroes to every kind of insolent lawlessness, to goad the people into acts of rebellion and resistance.

The other day in Charleston, which is under the command of that respectable creature General S——, they had a firemen's parade, and took the occasion to hoist a United States flag, to which this modern Gesler insisted on everyone raising his cap as he passed underneath. And by a hundred other such petty tyrannies are the people, bruised and sore, being roused to desperation; and had this been done directly after the war it would have been bad enough, but it was done the other day, three years after the close of the war.

The true reason is the desire and intention of the Government to control the elections of the South, which under the constitution of the country they could not legally do. So they have determined to make an excuse for setting aside the laws, and in order to accomplish this more fully, each commander in his separate district has issued an order declaring that unless a man can take an oath that he had not voluntarily borne arms against the

United States Government, nor in any way aided or abetted the rebellion, he cannot vote. This simply disqualifies every white man at the South from voting, disfranchising the whole white population, while the negroes are allowed to vote *en masse.*

This is particularly unjust, as the question of negro voting was introduced and passed in Congress as an amendment to the constitution, but in order to become a law a majority of two-thirds of the State Legislatures must ratify it, and so to them it was submitted, and rejected by all the Northern States with two exceptions, where the number of negro voters would be so small as to be harmless. Our Legislatures are not allowed to meet, but this law, which the North has rejected, is to be forced upon us, whose very heart it pierces and prosperity it kills. Meanwhile, in order to prepare the negroes to vote properly, stump speakers from the North are going all through the South, holding political meetings for the negroes, saying things like this to them : ' My

friends, you will have your rights, won't you ?'
(' Yes,' from the negroes.) 'Shall I not go
back to Massachusetts and tell your brothers
there that you are going to ride in the street
cars with white ladies if you please ?' (' Yes,
yes,' from the crowd.) 'That if you pay your
money to go to the theatre you will sit where
you please, in the best boxes if you like ?'
(' Yes,' and applause.) This I copy verbatim
from a speech made at Richmond the other
day, since which there have been two serious
negro riots there, and the General commanding had to call out the military to suppress
them.

These men are making a tour through
the South, speaking in the same way to the
negroes everywhere. Do you wonder we
are frightened ? I have been so forcibly
struck lately while reading Baker's 'Travels
in Africa,' and some of Du Chaillu's lectures,
at finding how exactly the same characteristics
show themselves among the negroes there, in
their own native country, where no outside

influences have ever affected them, as with ours here. Forced to work, they improve and are useful ; left to themselves they become idle and useless, and never improve. Hard ethnological facts for the abolitionists to swallow, but facts nevertheless.

It seems foolish to fill my letter to you with such matters, but all this comes home to us with such vital force that it is hard to write, or speak, or think of anything else, and the one subject that Southerners discuss whenever they meet is, 'What is to become of us ?'

Affectionately yours,

F——

I left the South for the North late in July, after a severe attack of fever brought on by my own imprudence. Just before I left an old negro died, named Carolina, one hundred years old. He had been my great grandfather's body servant, and my father was much attached to him, and sat up with him the night before he died, giving him extract of beef-tea every hour. My sister had sent us down two little jars as an experiment, and although it did not save poor old Carolina's life, I am sure it did mine, as it was the only nourishment I could get in the shape of animal food after my fever. When Carolina was buried in the beautiful and picturesque bit of land set apart for the negro burying-ground on the island, my father had a tombstone with the following inscription on it erected over him.

CAROLINA,

DIED JUNE 26, 1866,

AGED 100 YEARS.

A long life, marked by devotion to his Heavenly Father and fidelity to his earthly masters.

CHAPTER III.

1867–1868.

ALONE.

IN August of 1867 my father died, and as soon after as I was able I went down to the South to carry on his work, and to look after the negroes, who loved him so dearly and to whom he was so much attached. My brother-in-law went with me, and we reached Butler's Island in November. The people were indeed like sheep without a shepherd, and seemed dazed.

We had engaged a gentleman as overseer in Savannah, and appointed another our financial agent for the coming year, and besides this all my father's affairs were in the hands of an executor appointed by the Court to settle his estate, but before anything else could be done the negroes had to be settled with for the past two years, and their share of the crops divided according to the amount due to each man. My father had given each negro a little pass-book, in which had been entered from time to time the food, clothing, and money which each had received from him on account. Of these little books there were over three hundred, which represented their debits; then there was the large plantation ledger, in which an account of the work each man had, or had not, done every day for nearly two years, had been entered, which represented their credits. To the task of balancing these two accounts I set myself, wishing to feel sure that it was fairly done, and also because I knew the negroes would be more satisfied with my settlement.

Night after night, when the day's work was over, I sat up till two and three o'clock in the morning, going over and over the long

line of figures, and by degrees got them pretty
straight. I might have saved myself the
trouble. Not one negro understood it a bit,
but all were quite convinced they had been
cheated, most of them thinking that each man
was entitled to half the crop. I was so
anxious they should understand and see they
had been fairly dealt with, that I went over
and over again each man's account with him,
and would begin, 'Well, Jack (or Quash, or
Nero, as the case might be), you got on such
a date ten yards of homespun from your
master.' 'Yes, missus, massa gave me dat.'
'Then on such and such a day you had ten
dollars.' 'Yes, missus, dat so.' And so on
to the end of their debits, all of which they
acknowledged as just at once. (I have
thought since they were not clever enough to
conceive the idea of disputing that part of
the business.) When all these items were
named and agreed to, I read the total
amount, and then turned to the work account.
And here the trouble began, every man insist-

ing upon it that he had not missed one day
in the whole two years, and had done full
work each day. So after endless discussions,
which always ended just where they began, I
paid them the money due to them, which
was always received with the same remark,
'Well, well, work for massa two whole years,
and only get dis much.' Finding that their
faith in my father's justice never wavered, I
repeated and repeated and repeated, 'But I
am paying you from your master's own books
and accounts.' But the answer was always
the same, 'No, no, missus, massa not treat
us so.' Neither, oddly enough, did they seem
to think I wished to cheat them, but that I
was powerless to help matters, one man saying to me one day, 'You see, missus, a woman
ain't much 'count.' I learnt very soon how
useless all attempts at 'making them sensible'
(as they themselves express it) were, and
after a time, used to pay them their wages
and tell them to be off, without allowing any
of the lengthy arguments and discourses over

their payments they wished to indulge in, often more, I think, with an idea of asserting their independence and dignity, than from any real belief that they were not properly paid.

Their love for, and belief in my father, was beyond expression, and made me love them more than I can say. They never spoke of him without some touching and affection-ate expression that comforted me far more than words uttered by educated lips could have done. One old woman said, ' Missus, dey tell me dat at de North people have to pay to get buried. Massa pay no money here ; his own people nurse him, his own people bury him, and his own people grieve for him.' Another put some flowers in a tumbler by the grave; and another basin, water, and towels, saying, ' If massa's spirit come, I want him see dat old Nanny not forget how he call every morning for water for wash his hands ; ' and several of them used the expression in speaking of his death, ' Oh,

missus, our back jest broke.' No wonder I
loved them.

Their religion, although so mixed up
with superstition, was very real, and many
were the words of comfort I got from them.
One day, when I was crying, an old woman
put her arms round me and said, ' Missus,
don't cry ; it vex de Lord. I had tirteen
children, and I ain't got one left to put
even a coal in my pipe, and if I did not
trust de Lord Jesus, what would become of
me ? '

I am sorry to say, however, that finding
my intention was to alter nothing that my
father had arranged, some of them tried to
take advantage of it, one man assuring me
his master had given him a grove of orange
trees, another several acres of land, and so
on, always embellished with a story of his
own long and useful services, for which ' Massa
say, Boy, I gib you dis for your own.'

Notwithstanding their dissatisfaction at
the settlement, six thousand dollars was paid

out among them, many getting as much as two or three hundred apiece. The result was that a number of them left me and bought land of their own, and at one time it seemed doubtful if I should have hands at all left to work. The land they bought, and paid forty, fifty dollars and even more for an acre, was either within the town limits, for which they got no titles, and from which they were soon turned off, or out in the pine woods, where the land was so poor they could not raise a peck of corn to the acre. These lands were sold to them by a common class of men, principally small shopkeepers and Jews (the gentlemen refusing to sell their land to the negroes, although they occasionally rented it to them), and most frightfully cheated the poor people were. But they had got their land, and were building their little log cabins on it, fully believing that they were to live on their property and incomes the rest of their lives, like gentlemen.

The baneful leaven of politics had begun

working among them, brought to the South by the lowest set of blackguards who ever undertook the trade, making patriotism in truth the 'last refuge of a scoundrel,' as Dr. Johnson facetiously defines it, and themselves 'factious disturbers of the Government,' according to his equally pleasant definition of a patriot. Only in this case they came accredited from the Government, and the agent of the Freedmen's Bureau was our master, one always ready to believe the wildest complaints from negroes, and to call the whites to account for the same.

A negro carpenter complained that a gentleman owed him fifty dollars for work done, so without further inquiry or any trial, the agent sent the gentleman word to pay at once, *or* he would have him arrested, the sheriff at that time being one of his own former slaves. My brother-in-law, who was with me this year for a short time was a Northern man and a strong Republican in his feelings, this being the first visit he had ever paid to the South. But such a high-handed proceeding as this astonished him, and he expressed much indignation at it, and declared he would send an account of it to a Republican paper in Philadelphia, as the people at the North had no idea of the real state of things at the South. He had also expressed himself surprised and pleased at the courteous reception he had received, although known to be a Northerner, and also at the quietness of the country generally. I told him they would not publish his letter in the Philadelphia paper, and I was right, they did not.

A rather amusing incident occurred while he was with me. Having been in quiet possession of our property on St. Simon's Island for two years, we were suddenly notified one day, I never quite knew by whom, and in those days it was not easy always to know who our lawgivers were, that St. Simon's Island came under the head of abandoned property, being occupied by former owners, who, through contempt of the Government and President's authority, had refused to make application for its restoration under the law. ' Therefore,' so ran the order, 'such property shall be confiscated on the first day of January next, unless before that date the owners present themselves before the authorities (?), take the required oath of allegiance to the Government, and ask for its restoration.' This nothing would induce me to do, the whole thing was so preposterous, but my brother-in-law decided that under the circumstances it was better to obey. So he, a strong Republican, who had first voted for Lincoln and then for Grant, had never been at the South before in his life, and during the war had done all in his power to aid and support the Northern Government, even gallantly offering his services to his country when Pennsylvania was threatened by General Lee before the battle of Gettysburgh, had to go and take the oath of allegiance to the United States Government on

behalf of his wife's property, she also having
always sympathised with the Northern cause,
and having been so bitter in her feelings at
first as to refuse to receive a Southerner in
her house.

What a farce it was ! My brother-in-law
could not help being amused, it was such an
absurd position to find himself in, and he
declared it all came of ever putting his foot
in this miserable Southern country at all, and
he had no doubt the result would be that on
his return to the North he would find all his
Northern property confiscated, and be hung
as a rebel. He soon after left me, and then
my real troubles began. It seemed quite
hopeless ever to get the negroes to settle
down to steady work, and although they
still professed the greatest affection for and
faith in me, it certainly did not show itself
in works. My new agent assured me that
there must be a contract made and signed
with the negroes, binding them for a year, in
order to have any hold upon them at all, and

I am not sure that the Freedmen's Bureau
agent did not require such an agreement to
be drawn up and submitted to him for
approval before having it signed. Whether
they were right or not as regarded the hold
it gave us over the labourers I cannot say.
I think possibly it impressed them a little
more with the sense of their obligations, but
after having two of them run off in spite of
the solemnity of the contract, and having to
pay something like twenty dollars to the
authorities to fetch them back, we didn't
trouble ourselves much about enforcing it
after that.   At first the negroes flatly refused
to sign any contract at all, having been
advised by some of their Northern friends
not to do so, as it would put them back to
their former condition of slavery, and my
agents were quite powerless to make them
come to any terms.   So I determined to try
what my personal influence would accomplish.

The day before I was to have my inter-

view with the Butler's Island people, I
received a most cheerful note from Major
D——, saying that he had paid off all the
hands at St. Simon's, who seemed perfectly
satisfied, and were quite willing to contract
again for another year. I felt a little surprised at this, as it is not the negro's nature
to be satisfied with anything but plenty to
eat and idleness, but was rejoicing over the
news, when I was summoned to the office
to see six of the Hampton Point people who
had just arrived from St. Simon's. There they
were, one and all with exactly the same story
as the people here, reserved for my benefit as
their proper mistress and protector ; 'that
they had not received full credit for their
day's work, had been underpaid and over-
charged,' &c. &c., winding up with, 'Missus,
de people wait to see you down dere, and dey
won't sign de contract till you come.' 'But,'
said I, in despair, ' I can't possibly leave here
for a week at least, and the work must
begin there at once, or we shall get in no crop

this year.' But in vain; they merely said,
'We wait, missus, till you come.' 'Very well,'
I said, ' I'll go to-morrow. Only, mind you
are all there, for I must be back here the next
day to have this contract signed.'

The next morning, at a little after seven,
I started for St. Simon's in my small boat,
rowed by my two favourite men, reaching
there about ten, and taking Major D——
utterly by surprise, as he knew nothing of
what had happened. From the way the
negroes spoke the day before, one would
have supposed the mere sight of my face
would have done; but not one signed the
contract without a long argument on the
subject, most of them refusing to sign at all,
though they all assured me they wished to
work for me as long 'as de Lord spared
dem.' I knew, however, too well, that this
simply meant that they were willing to con-
tinue to live on St. Simon's as long as the
Lord spared them, but not to work, so I was
firm, and said, 'No, you must sign or go

away.' So one by one, with groans and sighs, they put their marks down opposite to their names, and by five I had them all in. At nine o'clock, on the first of the flood tide, I started back, reaching Butler's Island at midnight, nearly frozen, but found my maid, who really was everything to me that year, waiting for me with a blazing fire and hot tea ready to warm me.

The next morning at ten, I had the big mill bell rung to summon the people here to sign the contract, and then my work began in earnest. For six mortal hours I sat in the office without once leaving my chair, while the people poured in and poured out, each one with long explanations, objections, and demonstrations. I saw that even those who came fully intending to sign would have their say, so after interrupting one man and having him say gravely, ' 'Top, missus, don't cut my discourse,' I sat in a state of dogged patience and let everyone have his talk out, reading the contract over and over again as

each one asked for it, answering their many
questions and meeting their many objections
as best I could. One wanted this altered
in the contract, and another that. One was
willing to work in the mill but not in the
field. Several would not agree to sign unless I promised to give them the whole
of Saturday for a holiday. Others, like the
St. Simon's people, would 'work for me till
they died,' but would put their hand to no
paper. And so it went on all day, each one
'making me sensible,' as he called it.

But I was immovable. 'No, they must
sign the contract as it stood.' 'No, I could
not have anyone work without signing.' 'No,
they must work six days and rest on Sunday,'
&c., &c. Till at last, six o'clock in the
evening came and I closed the books with
sixty-two names down, which was a good
deal of a triumph, as my agent told me he
feared none would sign the contract, they
were so dissatisfied with last year's settlement. Even old Henry, one of the captains,

and my chief friend and supporter, said in
the morning, ' Missus, I bery sorriful, for half
de people is going to leave.' ' Oh no, they
won't, Henry,' said I. But I thought sixty-
two the first day, good work, though I had
a violent attack of hysterics afterwards, from
fatigue and excitement. Only once did I
lose my temper and self-control, and that was
when one man, after showing decided signs
of insolence, said, ' Well, you sign my paper
first, and then I'll sign yours.' ' No,' I
replied in a rage, ' I'll neither sign yours nor
you mine. Go out of the room and off the
place instantly.' But I soon saw how foolish
I was, for looking up five minutes after, I
beheld the same man standing against the
door with a broad grin on his face, who,
when I looked at him in perfect astonishment,
said with the most perfect good nature, ' I'se
come back to sign, missus.'

The next day, Sunday, I tried to keep
clear of the people, both for rest and because
I wanted to make some arrangements for my

school, the young teacher having arrived on Friday.

Monday morning the bell again rang, and though I did not see more than twenty-five people, I was again in the office from ten A.M. to six P.M., and found it far more unpleasant than on Saturday, as I had several trouble-some, bad fellows to deal with. One man, who proposed leaving the place without pay-ing his debts, informed me, when I told him he must pay first, ' he'd see if he hadn't a law as well as I ; ' and another positively refused to work or leave the place, so he had to be informed that if he was not gone in three days he would be put off, which had such an effect that he came the next day and signed, and worked well afterwards.

Tuesday and Wednesday my stragglers came dropping in, the last man arriving under a large cotton umbrella, very defiant that he would not sign unless he could have Satur-day for a holiday. ' Five days I'll work, but (with a flourish of the umbrella) I works

for no man on Saturday.' 'Then,' said I,
'William, I am sorry, but you can't work for
me, for any man who works for me *must*
work on Saturday.' 'Good morning, den,
missus,' says my man, with another flourish
of the umbrella, and departs. About an hour
afterwards he returned, much subdued, with
the umbrella shut, which I thought a good
sign, and informed me that after 'much
consideration wid himself,' he had returned
to sign. So that ended it, and only two men
really went—one from imagined ill-health,
and one I dismissed for insubordination.
The gentlemen seemed to think I had done
wonders, and I was rather astonished at
myself, but nothing would ever induce me to
do such a thing again.

The backbone of the opposition thus
broken, and the work started more or less
steadily, I turned my thoughts to what I
considered my principal work, and belonging
more to my sphere than what I had been
engaged in up to that time. I was anxious

to have the negroes' houses, which were
terribly dilapidated, repaired and whitewashed, a school opened, and the old hospital
building repaired and put in order for the
following purposes. One of the four big
rooms the people had taken possession of
for a church, the old one being some three
miles distant, at one of the upper settlements,
and this I determined to let them keep, and
to use one of the others for the school ; one
for the old women who couldn't work, and
the other for the young married women to
be confined in, as, since the war, they bring
their children into the world anyhow and
anywhere, in their little cabins, where men,
women, and children run in and out indiscriminately, so that it is both wretched and
improper.

The people did not seem to like either
of my proposals too much ; especially the old
plantation midwife, who is indignant at her
work being taken away from her. But as I
find she now makes the charge of five dollars

for each case, the negroes naturally decline employing her on their own account. I hoped by degrees to bring them to approve of my arrangements, by showing them how much more comfortable they would be in my hospital, and by presenting the babies born there with some clothes, and the old women who lived there with blankets, to make them like it. (I never did succeed, however, and after several attempts, had to give it up.)

I had one or two pupils at the same time, and found the greatest difference between the genuine full-blooded African and the mulattoes. The first, although learning to repeat quickly, like a clever parrot, did not really take in an idea, while the other was as intelligent as possible. I felt sure then, and still think, the pure negro incapable of advancement to any degree that would enable him to cope with the white race, intellectually, morally, or even physically. My white maid took infinite pains to show them

the best, quickest, as well as simplest way of
doing the house-work, absolutely taking their
breath away by the way she worked herself,
but without much effect, as the instant her
back was turned they went back to their old
lazy, slipshod ways of doing things. Her
efforts to make them tidy in their dress were
very amusing, and one morning, finding my
young housemaid working with her sun-
bonnet on, I said, 'Why do you keep your
bonnet on, Christine?' Upon which, without
any reply, she pulled the said bonnet down
over her eyes, and my maid informed me
she had come to work in the morning without brushing her hair, so for punishment had
to wear her sun-bonnet. The women showed
a strong inclination to give up wearing their
pretty, picturesque head handkerchiefs, ' because white people didn't,' but I was very
strict about the house servants never coming
without one on, for their black woolly heads
did look too ugly without their usual covering, which in itself was so handsome, and

gave them so much style, and in some cases beauty.

A few days after the contract was signed I started the school, which I hoped would be a success. The teacher was a young country lad just fresh from college ; clever enough, but very conceited, with no more manners than a young bear, which, however, I hoped he might learn in time from the negroes in return for some book learning, as they generally are singularly gentle and courteous in their manners. I had school in the morning for the children, and in the evening for the young people who worked in the fields. This is decidedly the most popular, and we have over fifty scholars, some of them quite old men—much too old to learn, and much in the way of the younger ones, but so zealous that I could not bear to turn them away.

Besides teaching school, my young man was to take charge of the store, which I found too much for me. My father's object in opening the store was to give the negroes good things at cost price, in order to save them from paying three times the price for most inferior goods in Darien, where a number of small shops had been opened. But we did not take into consideration the heavy loss it must entail upon us not to put even profit enough on the things to cover our own expenses, and we sold them to the negroes at exactly what we paid for them in Philadelphia, bearing all the cost of transportation and spoilt goods, so that at the end of the following year I found the store just three thousand dollars out of pocket, and so decided to shut it up, especially as I found that, notwithstanding our giving the negroes the very best things at cost price, they much preferred going to Darien to spend their money on inferior goods and at greatly increased rates. I suppose, poor people, it was natural they should like to swagger a little, and spend their newly, but certainly not hardly-earned money freely, and it was an immense relief to my pocket and labours to give up shop-keeping, although we only had it open for about two hours every afternoon.

But all this time, while we were getting things more and more settled on the place, the troubles from outside were drawing nearer and nearer as the day for voting approached, and in March burst upon us in the shape of political meetings and excitement of all kinds. Two or three Northern political agents arrived in Darien, and summoned all the negroes to attend meetings, threatening them with various punishments if they stayed away. I in vain reasoned with the negroes, and did all in my power to prevent their attending these meetings, and told them no one could punish them for not going : not because I cared in the least which way they voted, but because it interfered so terribly with their work. I doubled the watchmen at night, and did all I could to prevent strangers land-ing on the Island ; but one morning found that during the night a notice had been put

up on the wharf, calling upon all the people
to attend a political meeting on pain of being
fined five hundred dollars, or exiled to a
foreign land. As the meeting was some way
off, and the election followed in a few days,
I knew that if the people once broke off, no
more work would be done for at least a week,
and this was just the time one of our plant-
ings had to be put in, which, as we can only
do it on the spring tides, would have cost
me just two hundred acres of rice. So I
argued and threatened, and told them it was
all rubbish—no one could either exile or
fine them, and that they must not go to the
meeting at all, and when the day for voting
came must do all their day's work first and
vote afterwards; which they easily could
have done, having always finished their day's
work by three o'clock, and the voting place
not being half a mile off.

It was useless, however. My words were
powerless, the negroes naturally thinking
that the people who had freed them could

do anything they liked, and must be obeyed ;
so they not only prepared to go to the meeting, but, I knew, would not do a stroke of
work on the voting days. At last, in despair,
I wrote to General Meade, who was then
the military commander of our district, and
a personal acquaintance of mine, to tell him
what was going on, and ask him if it was
impossible that the planters should be protected from these political disturbers and
agitators. I received the following answer
and order from him almost immediately :—

Head-quarters, Third Military District.
(Department of Georgia, Florida, and Alabama.)
Atlanta, Georgia : April 11, 1868.

My dear Miss B——,—I have to acknowledge the receipt of your letter, reporting
that certain persons are ordering the labourers
under your employment to attend political
meetings, and threatening, in case of refusal,
to punish them with fines or exile them to a
foreign country ; and have to state in reply,
that no interference of any kind with the

just rights of employers is authorised by existing laws or orders, and that, on the contrary, you will see, from the enclosed order, which was being prepared at the time your letter was received, that such interference is positively prohibited, and is punishable on conviction before a military tribunal with fine and imprisonment. If you will furnish these Head-quarters with the names of parties thus attempting to interfere with your rights as an employer, together with the names of reliable witnesses, I shall not hesitate to investigate the case, and bring the offenders to trial and punishment.

Very respectfully yours,
George G. Meade,
Major-General.

The order was as follows :—

Head-quarters, Third Military District.
(Department of Georgia, Florida, and Alabama.)

General Orders, No. 58.—The uncertainty which seems to exist in regard to holding municipal elections on the 20th inst., and the frequent inquiries addressed to these Head-quarters, renders it necessary for the commanding General to announce that said elections are not authorised by any orders from these Head-quarters. Managers of elections are hereby prohibited from receiving any votes, except such State and county offices as are provided for in the constitution, to be submitted for ratification, the voting for which offices is authorised by General Orders, Nos. 51 and 52.

No. 2. Complaints having been made to these Head-quarters, by planters and others, that improper means are being used to compel labourers to leave their work to attend political meetings, and threats being made that in case of refusal penalties will be attached to said refusal, the Major-General Commanding announces that all such attempts to control the movements of labourers and interfere with the rights of employers are strictly forbidden and will be considered, and, on conviction, will be punished, the same as any attempt to dissuade voters from going to the polls, as referred to in paragraph 11, General Orders, No. 57.

No. 3. The Major-General Commanding also makes known that, while he acknowledges, and will require to be respected, the right of labourers to peacefully assemble at night to discuss political questions, yet he discountenances and forbids the assembling of armed bodies, and requires that all such assemblages shall notify either the civil or military authorities of these proposed meetings, and said military and civil authorities are enjoined to see that the right of electors to peaceably assemble for legitimate purposes is not disturbed.

No. 4. The wearing or carrying of arms, either concealed or otherwise, by persons not connected with the military service of the Government, or such civil officers whose duties under the laws and orders is to preserve the public peace, at or in the vicinity of the polling places, on the days set apart for holding the election in the State of Georgia, is positively forbidden. Civil and military officers will see that this order, as well as all others relative to the preservation of the peace and quiet of the counties in which they are acting, is strictly observed.

By order of Major-General MEADE,

R. C. DRUM, A.A.G.

These orders were accompanied by a private letter, which was as follows :—

Easter Sunday : April 11, 1868.

My dear Miss B——,—You will see by my writing you to-day how much I feel flattered by your appeal to me, and how ready I am to respond to it. I regret very much to learn the state of affairs as described by you ; they are certainly unauthorised by any laws or orders from these Head-quarters, and, since the receipt of your letter I have had prepared an order to cover such case, and forbidding the interference of political agents with the rights of employers. I will have a copy sent to you officially, which you can make use of to correct this evil in future.

I have been twice in Savannah, on my way to Florida; have both times thought of you and inquired after you. If you had been a little more accessible, and had I not feared to compromise you by a visit from the awful military satrap and despot who rules so tyrannically over you, Miss W——will tell you that I, as well as the Colonel (my son), were both desirous of visiting you. I am very much gratified to learn that you acknowledge being my subject, and beg you to remember the acknowledgment is reciprocal, as I acknowledge my allegiance to you—an allegiance founded on respect, kindly regard, and many pleasant recollections of former times.

Let me assure you I shall be ready at all times to aid and encourage you in your labours, and that you must not hesitate to appeal to me ; for, though many people will not believe it, I am trying to act impartially, and to do justice to all.

Very truly and sincerely yours,

GEORGE G. MEADE.

P.S.—Your letter being marked private, I have not deemed myself justified in acting on it, but you will see from my official letter that, if you will send me evidence and names of witnesses in Mr. Campbell's case, I will attend to that gentleman. Official letter goes by to-day's mail with this. Let me know if it does not reach you.

I was, of course, much pleased and very triumphant when I received these letters, although it was impossible to comply with General Meade's request that we would report the offenders, as the notices served on the negroes were never signed—which convinced us of their illegality, but did not in the least take away from their importance

to the negroes. Still, I not only read my
order to them, but had it posted up in
Darien, and, on the strength of it, repeated
my previous orders to my negroes that, if
one of them neglected his work to attend
political meetings or to vote, I would dismiss
him from the place; adding, at the same
time, 'there is no difficulty about your
voting after your work is over.' My surprise
and disgust were therefore extreme when I
received the following day a second letter
from General Meade, as follows :—

Atlanta : April 13, 1868.

My dear Miss B——,—I wrote you
very hastily yesterday on my return from
church, not wishing to lose a mail, advising
you of my views and action. I find to-day,
on a careful re-perusal of your letter, that you
are in error in one particular. You seem to
think you have the right to decide when your
people shall vote, and that as there is time
for them after three o'clock, the end of their
day's work, that you are authorised to pro-

hibit their leaving at an earlier hour. This is not so, and I would advise you not to insist on it. The theory of my order is that no restraint is to be put on the labourer to prevent his voting.

Now as it is sometimes difficult for a person to vote as soon as he reaches the polls, some having to wait days for their turn, and as, often, examination has to be made of the registration books, and the voter in addition to the delay of awaiting his turn after getting up to the polls, may find some error in the spelling of his name or omission to put his name on the list, and in consequence of these obstacles lose his turn to have the error corrected and then again take his chance, more time must be allowed than your rule would admit. I think you will have to make up your mind that the election will be a great nuisance, and that you will not get much out of your people during its continuance. If they are reasonable and the facilities good at Darien, they should not

require any more time than is absolutely
necessary, but as I know that voting is a
work of time, for which reason we give
four days, I fear these plausible, and perhaps
actual obstacles, will be taken advantage of
to spend the time in idleness and frolicking,
on the plea that ' they could not get a chance
to vote.'

I take the liberty of writing this to you
because my letter of yesterday might lead
you astray.   Again assuring you of my warm
regard,

I remain,
Yours very truly,
GEORGE G. MEADE.

I naturally felt indignant at this letter,
for I had told General Meade that I did not
intend to interfere with my negroes voting,
but only to save myself from loss, and in my
case no difficulty existed about their reaching
the polls, which were not a mile from the house.
And this second letter undid all the good of

the first, besides which I could not help
feeling the gross injustice of coolly telling me
that for four whole days I must not expect
any work, for it would really just in that
week have entailed a loss of two hundred
acres, as I told General Meade in my letter.
And what Northern farmer or manufacturer
would have submitted for one moment to an
order from the Government, directing him to
give his employés four whole days for voting,
just at the busiest season ?

I was both hurt and angry, and never
have to this day understood this afterthought
of General Meade. He was always so kind
and courteous, and had been a personal friend
of my father, and could not really have dis-
believed my statements. I suppose that he
thought in fact I was not my own mistress,
but acting under orders and advice from my
Southern neighbours. But I can solemnly
assert that neither then nor since, to my
knowledge, have my negroes been influenced
in their way of voting by the planters, beyond

a mere joking remark as to whether they felt
sure that they had the right ticket, or some
such thing. I think most of the gentlemen
felt as I did, that the negroes voting at all
was such a wicked farce that it only deserved
our contempt. I do not say that no outside
influence was ever used afterwards, although
I do not know of any personally, and certainly, no intimidation, as I think I can most
clearly and satisfactorily prove by a statement
as to how matters stand with us politically at
present. From first to last all our political
disturbances arose from agents belonging to
the Republican party, mostly Northern adventurers, of whom, thank God, we are now
rid.

After thinking the matter over I determined to pay no attention to General Meade's
second letter, as I felt I was justified in doing
by the facts of the case. So I put the letter
in my pocket, and repeated my orders that
the negroes were to do their work first, and
vote afterwards.

The election day came, and my agent, who was not very judicious and was very excitable, had me awaked at six o'clock in the morning to tell me that there was not a negro in the field, all having announced their intention of going over to Darien to vote. By ten o'clock there was not a man left on the place, even the old half-idiot, who took care of the cows, having gone to vote with the rest; and my agent, who was much excited over it all, said, ' Now, Miss B——, what will you do ? You can't dismiss the whole plantation.' I confess for a moment I felt checkmated, and did not know what to do, but as I had intended to go down to St. Simon's that day I determined to carry out my intention, which would give me time to think quietly and coolly over the situation. So I sent word to my two boat hands that they must cast their votes as soon as possible and return to take me down, an order they promptly obeyed. The next day I received a note from my agent, saying that the hands had all returned to their work early in the day after voting, and had all finished the entire task with the exception of two or three, who promised to do double work the next day. Here was an unexpected triumph, and I truly believe that my plantation was almost the only one in the whole State of Georgia where any work was done during those four days, and apart from the actual loss of labour, four days of idleness would have made it doubly difficult to get the people in hand again. Down on St. Simon's their ardour about voting was considerably cooled by the fact that they had twelve miles to walk to the polls, and besides had not been visited by any political agents to stir them up. So only a few out of the whole number went, and we had no trouble about it. This ended our political troubles for this year, but the work was still anything but steady or satisfactory, and hardly a day passed without difficulty in some shape or other.

In a letter written at the end of April I say :—

All winter I have had a sort of feeling that before long I should get through and have things settled ; but I am beginning to find out that there is no getting through here, for just as you are about getting through, you have to begin all over again. I have had a good deal of trouble this last week with my people— not serious, but desperately wearisome. They are the most extraordinary creatures, and the mixture of leniency and severity which it is requisite to exercise in order to manage them is beyond belief. Each thing is explained satisfactorily to them and they go to work. Suddenly some one, usually the most stupid, starts an idea that perhaps by-and-by they may be expected to do a little more work, or be deprived of some privilege ; upon which the whole field gets in the most excited state, they put down their hoes and come up to the house for another explanation, which lasts till the same thing happens again.

They are the most effervescent people in the world, and to see them in one of their excitements, gesticulating wildly, talking so violently that no one on earth can understand one word they say, you would suppose they never could be brought under control again. But go into the field the next morning, and there they are, as quiet, peaceable, and cheerful as if nothing had happened. At first I used to talk too, but now I just stand perfectly quiet until they have talked themselves out, and then I ask some simple question which shows them how foolish they have been, and they cool down in a moment.

The other day, while I was at dinner, I heard tramp, tramp, outside, and a gang of fifty arrived, the idea having occurred to them that, while I was gone in harvest time, they might be overworked. They talked and they raved 'that they had contracted to do two tasks and no more,' going from one imaginary grievance to another, until one man suddenly broke out with, 'And, missus, when we work night and day, we ought to be paid extra.' Upon which they all took it up,

'Yes, missus, when we tired with working hard all day, den to work all night for nothing is too much.' Not having spoken before, I then said very quietly, ' Have you ever been asked to work at night ?' There was a dead pause for a moment, and then one man said rather sheepishly, ' No.' 'Well,' said I, ' when you are, you will certainly be paid extra, and now, as you seem to have forgotten the contract, I will read it to you over again.'

So I brought it out and read it slowly and solemnly, dwelling particularly on the part in which it said, ' The undersigned freed men and women agree to obey all orders and to do the work required of them in a satisfactory manner, and in event of any violation of this contract, they are to be dismissed the place and to forfeit all wages due to them.' This cooled them considerably, and when I added, ' Now understand, your work is just what you are told to do, and if one bushel of rice is lost through your disobedience

or carelessness, you shall pay for it,' this
quenched them utterly, and they went to
work the next morning with the greatest
possible good-will, and all will go on well
until the next time, whenever that may be.
But what with troubles without and troubles
within, life is a burden and rice a difficult
crop to raise.

As for Mr. D——'s and Mr. W——'s
opinions about the glorious future of our Sea
Island cotton plantations, they are worth just
as much as the paper on which their calcula-
tions are made, and are theoretical entirely.

Mr. G——, another rich New York man,
who figured it all out on paper there, came
here two years ago to make his fortune, and
he told me the other day that he was perfectly
convinced that Sea Island cotton never would
pay again. Rice, he said, might, but this fine
cotton, never. The expense and risk of raising it was too great, and the price too much
lowered by foreign competition. The labour
is too uncertain, and anyone who knows, as I

do, that after all my hard work the crop may be lost at any moment by the negroes going off or refusing to work, knows how useless it is to count on any returns with certainty. Wherever white labour can be introduced, other crops will be cultivated, and wherever it can't, the land will remain uncultivated.

Rice lands now rent at ten dollars an acre, and cotton from two to three, so you can judge what the people here think about it; and, after all, I suppose they must know best. The orange trees are all in full bloom now, and smell most deliciously sweet, and the little place looks its prettiest, which is not saying much for it, it is true. Another year I hope to improve it by removing the negro houses away from where they now are, close to this house, to where I can neither see, hear, nor smell them. I shall then run my own fence out a little further, taking in a magnificent magnolia and some large orange trees, which, with the quantities of flowers I have set out everywhere, will at any rate make the garden round the house pretty.

A little later on, the Island being submerged by a sudden overflow and rise of the river, I accepted an invitation from some friends in South Carolina, also rice-planters, to visit them. From there I write as follows :—

Mrs. P.'s family consists of a very nice girl about my own age, clever and well-educated, and two sons, one about twenty-seven and the other about twenty-four, both of whom were educated abroad, and are well-informed and intelligent. So altogether it is a pleasant family to be in, and as we are all trying to make our fortunes as rice-planters, we have everything in common, and talk 'rice' all day.

I have ridden every day since I have been here, and on Friday went deer-hunting, which, of course, I enjoyed very much. We started at eight o'clock in the morning, and did not return till five o'clock in the afternoon, having seen six deer and killed two, one of which we lost, after a short run, in the river.

This part of the country has suffered more heavily than any other from the war. Hundreds of acres of rice land, which yielded millions before the war, are fast returning to the original swamp from which they were reclaimed with infinite pains and expense, simply because their owners are ruined, their houses burnt to the ground, and their negroes made worthless as labourers. It is very sad to see such wide-spread ruin, and to hear of girls well-educated, and brought up with every luxury, turned adrift as dressmakers, schoolteachers, and even shop girls, in order to keep themselves and their families from starvation. One of Mrs. F——'s nieces paddles her old father over to the plantation every morning herself, and while he is giving his orders in the fields, sits on a heap of straw, making underclothes to sell in Charleston. It is wonderful to me to see how bravely and cheerfully they

do work, knowing as I do how they lived
before the war.

I was agreeably surprised with the beauty
of this place, for I thought all rice plantations,
like Butler's Island, were ugly and uninter-
esting. Here the rice fields are quite out of
sight. The garden, which is very large, is
enclosed by a lovely hedge of some sweet-
smelling shrub and roses ; in it are clematis
and sweet olea bushes thirty feet high, with
quantities of violets and all sorts of sweet
things besides. Then there are three superb
live oak trees, from under which we look out
on the river, which runs clear and deep in
front of the house. The house itself is a good-
sized building, with remains of great elegance
about it, and with some nice old family pic-
tures and china in it. Mrs. P—— is very
proud of having saved these things, which
she did by remaining with her daughter in
the house during a raid, when all her neighbours fled, leaving their houses to be literally
emptied of their contents by the soldiers of

the Northern army who visited this section of the country.

M—— told me a funny story of a visit she received from a tipsy Yankee captain, to whom she and her mother were, from interested motives, most civil, and who became so affected by her charms that he presented her with a silver pitcher to which he had just helped himself from a neighbouring house, which she gratefully accepted, and returned as soon as possible to its rightful owner.

I leave here this evening, as my agent writes me the waters have subsided from the face of the earth. So I must get back to my work and to my new planting machine, which I am very anxious to try, being the first step towards freeing ourselves from negro labourers.

On my return, the season being well advanced and the rice place no longer healthy, I went down at once to the cotton plantation, of which my final letter written from the South this year gives this account :——

Hampton Point : May 5, 1868.

I came down here last Tuesday, as, before I return to the North I want to get a little sea air, as well as to have the house re-shingled, the rain now coming through the old roof in plentiful showers. The main body of the house, I am glad to find, is perfectly good, so that repairing the roof and piazzas will put it in thorough order; and as I have brought my whole force of eight carpenters down, the work is going briskly forward. This place, always lovely, is now looking its best, with all the young spring greens and flowers lighting up the woods, and I long to cut and trim, lay out and take up, making the place as beautiful as it is capable of being made. It is a great contrast in every way to Butler's Island, the place as well as people.

The proximity of the other place to Darien has a very demoralising effect upon the negroes there. Here everything moves on steadily and quietly, as it used to do in old

times. Bram still has charge, and with his
three nice grown sons, gives the tone to the
place. We have planted about a hundred
and twenty-five acres of cotton, all of which
are coming up well and healthy. But this time
last year it looked well too, and then, alas!
alas! was totally destroyed by the army-
worm, so who can tell if it may not again be
swept from off the face of the earth in a single
night, as it was last year.

Your notion, and Miss F——'s, that the
negroes ought at once to be made to realise
their new condition and position, is an impossibility, and you might just as well expect
children of ten and eleven to suddenly realise
their full responsibilities as men and women,
as these people. That they will come to it
in time I hope and believe, and for that
purpose I am having them educated, trying
to increase their desire for comforts, and
excite their ambition to furnish their houses
and make them neat and pretty. But the
change was too great to expect them to adopt

the new state of things at once, and they must come to it by degrees, during which time my personal influence is necessary to keep them up in their work, and to prevent them falling into habits of utter worthlessness, from which they can never be reclaimed.

From the first, the fixed notion in their minds has been that liberty meant idleness, and they must be forced to work until they become intelligent enough to know the value of labour. As for starving them into this, that is impossible too, for it is a well-known fact that you can't starve a negro. At this moment there are about a dozen on Butler's Island who do no work, consequently get no wages and no food, and I see no difference whatever in their condition and those who get twelve dollars a month and full rations. They all raise a little corn and sweet potatoes, and with their facilities for catching fish and oysters, and shooting wild game, they have as much to eat as they want, and now are quite satisfied with that, not yet having learned to want things that money alone can give.

The proof that my theory about personal influence is the only means at present by which the people can be managed, is that my father, by his strong influence over them last year, made the best crop that was raised in the country, and this year our people are working far better than others in the neighbourhood, and we have again the prospect of a large crop, while our neighbours are in despair, their hands running off, refusing to work, and even in some places raising riots in the place. Not that their masters are not paying them their wages, for in some cases they are giving them more than we do ; but because they just pay them off so much a month and trouble their heads no more about them, just as if they were white labourers. Now, my desire and object is to put them on this footing as soon as possible, but they must be kept in leading-strings until they are able to stand alone.

CHAPTER IV.

1868–1869.

RECONSTRUCTION.

IN November of the same year I again visited the South, having received during the summer one or two sensational telegrams from my agent, who was apt to lose his head, and although they sounded very alarming, they proved to be the creation of a vivid imagination or unfounded reports, and on the whole the people had done very well, and we had a large crop for the acreage planted. This year I took a friend with me, and my maid. Christmas, politics, and paying-off had again upset all the negroes, and many of them said they intended to leave the place, and some did. We were now giving 12 dollars a month, with rations, half the money being paid at the end of every month, and the rest, at the end of the year. Knowing that it was quite useless to try and get them to settle down until after the first of the year, I let them alone and devoted myself to the children, for whom I had a beautiful Christmas tree. I wrote on Christmas evening an account of it all.

Christmas 1868.

Dearest M——, You have heard of our safe arrival, and how much more comfortable the travelling was than last year. We arrived about a month ago, and I have been hard at work ever since. The negroes do not seem to be in a very satisfactory condition, but it is owing in a great measure, I think, to its being Christmas time. They are all prepared again to make their own, and different, terms for next year, but except for the bother and trouble I don't feel very anxious about it, for we have a gang of Irishmen doing the

banking and ditching, which the negroes
utterly refuse to do any more at all, and
therefore, until the planting begins, we can
do without the negro labour.

Last year they humbugged me completely
by their expressions of affection and desire to
work for me, but now that the novelty of
their getting back once more to their old
home has entirely worn off and they have
lost their old habits of work, the effects of
freedom are beginning to tell, and everywhere
sullen unwillingness to work is visible, and all
round us people are discussing how to get
other labourers in the place of negroes.   But
alas! on the rice lands white labour is impossible, so that I really don't know what we shall
do, and I think things look very gloomy for
the planters. Our Northern neighbours on St.
Simon's, the D——s, who were most hopeful
last year, are now perfectly discouraged with
the difficulties they have to encounter with
their labour, and of course having to lose two
or three months every year while the negroes

are making up their minds whether they will work or not, obliges us to plant much less ground than we should otherwise do. However, there is no use taking evil on account, and when we are ruined will be time enough to say free labour here is a failure, and I still hope that when their Christmas excitement is over, the people will settle down to work.

My Christmas tree this afternoon was a great success; it was really very pretty. I had three rooms packed full of people, the women begging me to give them dolls and the toys, which I had brought of course for the children alone. The orange trees are a miracle of beauty; many of the branches touch the ground from the weight of the fruit, and you cannot walk under them without knocking the oranges with your head. Several of the trees have yielded two thousand, and the whole crop is estimated at sixteen thousand.

We had a small excitement about this

K

time, owing to a report which went the round of the plantations, that there was to be a general negro insurrection on the 1st of the year. I did not much believe it, but as I had promised my friends at the North, who were very anxious about me, to run no risks and to take every precaution against danger, I thought it best to seek some means of protection. I first asked my friend whether she felt nervous and would rather leave the Island, but she, being a true soldier's daughter, said no, she would stay and take her chance with me. We then agreed to say nothing about it to my maid, who was a new English maid, thinking that if we did not mind having *our* throats cut, neither need she—particularly as she now spent most of her time weeping at the horrors which surrounded her.

I wrote therefore to our nearest military station and asked that a guard of soldiers might be sent over for a day or two, which was done. But as they came without any officer, and conducted themselves generally disagreeably, stealing the oranges, worrying the negroes, and making themselves entirely at home even to the point of demanding to be fed by me, I packed them off, preferring to take my chance with my negroes than with my protectors. I don't believe that there was the least foundation for the report of the insurrection, but we had trouble enough the whole winter in one form or other.

The negroes this year and the following seemed to reach the climax of lawless independence, and I never slept without a loaded pistol by my bed. Their whole manner was changed ; they took to calling their former owners by their last name without any title before it, constantly spoke of my agent as old R———, dropped the pleasant term of ' Mistress,' took to calling me ' Miss Fanny,' walked about with guns upon their shoulders, worked just as much and when they pleased, and tried speaking to me with their hats on, or not touching them to me when they passed me on the banks. This last rudeness I never permitted for a moment, and always said sharply, 'Take your hat off instantly,' and was obliged to take a tone to them generally which I had never done before. One or two, who seemed rather more inclined to be insolent than the rest, I dismissed, always saying, 'You are free to leave the place, but not to stay here and behave as you please, for I am free too, and moreover own the place, and so have a right to give my orders on it, and have them obeyed.'

I felt sure that if I relaxed my discipline for one moment all was up, and I never could control the negroes or plant the place again ; and to this unerring rule I am sure I owe my success, although for that year, and the two following, I felt the whole time that it was touch-and-go whether I or the negroes got the upper hand.

A new trouble came upon us too, or

rather an old trouble in a new shape. Negro adventurers from the North, finding that politics was such a paying trade at the South, began pouring in, and were really worse than the whites, for their Southern brethren looked upon their advent quite as a proof of a new order of things, in which the negroes were to rule and possess the land.

We had a fine specimen in one Mr. Tunis Campbell, whose history is rather peculiar. Massachusetts had the honour of giving him birth, and on his first arrival in Georgia he established himself, whether with or without permission I know not, on St. Catherine's Island, a large island midway between Savannah and Darien, which was at that time deserted. The owner, without returning, rented it to a Northern party, who on coming to take possession found Mr. Campbell established there, who declined to move, on some pretended permission he had from the Government to occupy it, and it was necessary to apply to the authorities at Darien to remove him, which was done by sending a small armed force. He then came to Darien, and very soon became a leader of the negroes, over whom he acquired the most absolute control, and managed exactly as he pleased, so that when the first vote for State and county authorities was cast, he had no difficulty in having himself elected a magistrate, and for several years administered justice with a high hand and happy disregard of law, there being no one to oppose him.

Happily, he at last went a little too far, and arrested the captain of a British vessel, which had come to Darien for timber, for assault and battery, because he pushed Campbell's son out of the way on the deck of his own ship. The captain was brought before Campbell, tried, and sentenced to pay a heavy fine, from which he very naturally appealed to the English Consul in Savannah, who of course ordered his release at once. This and some other equally lawless acts by which Mr. Campbell was in the habit of filling his own pockets, drew the attention of the authorities to him, and a very good young judge having just been put on our circuit, he was tried for false imprisonment, and sentenced to one year's imprisonment himself, which not only freed us from his iniquitous rule, against which we had had no appeal, but broke the spell which he held over the negroes, who up till the time of his downfall, had believed his powers omnipotent, and at his instigation had defied all other authority ; which state of things had driven the planters to despair, for there seemed to be no remedy for this evil, the negroes throwing all our authority to the wind, and following Campbell wherever he chose to lead them.

So desperate were some of the gentlemen, that at one time they entertained the idea of seeing if they could not buy Campbell over, and induce him by heavy bribes to work for us, or rather to use his influence over our negroes to make them work for us. And this proposition was made to me, but I could not consent to such a plan. In the first place it was utterly opposed to my notions of what was right, and my pride revolted from the idea of making any such bargain with a creature like Campbell ; besides which I felt sure it was bad policy, that if we bought him one day he would sell us the next. So I refused to have anything to do with the project, and it was fortunately never carried out, for although during the next three or four years Campbell gave us infinite trouble, he would have given us far more had we put ourselves in his power by offering him a bribe.

My agent unfortunately was not much assistance to me, being nervous, timid, and irresolute. Naturally his first thought was to raise the crops by any means that he could, but feeling himself powerless to enforce his orders, owing to the fact that we had no proper authorities to appeal to, should our negroes misbehave themselves, these representatives of the Government pandering to the negroes in every way, in order to secure their votes for themselves, he was obliged to resort to any means he could, to get any work out of the negroes at all, often changing his tactics and giving different orders from day to day. In vain I implored him to be firm, and if he gave an order to stand to it ; but the invariable answer was, ' It's of no use, Miss B——, I should only get myself into trouble, and have the negro sheriff sent over by Campbell to arrest me.' And everyone went on the same principle. One of the negroes committed a brutal murder, but no notice was taken of it by any of the authorities, until, with much personal trouble, I had him arrested and shut up. Shortly afterwards, greatly to my astonishment and indignation, I met him walking about the place, and on inquiring how he had got out, was coolly informed that ' a gentleman had hired him, from the agent of the Freedmen's Bureau, to work on his plantation.' I went at once to the agent, and told him that if the man was not re-arrested at once and kept confined, I would report him to the higher authorities.

A few days afterwards I visited the same negro in his prison (!) which turned out to be a deserted warehouse, with no fastening upon the door, and here I found him playing the fiddle to a party who were dancing. He did meet his fate however, poor fellow, at last, but not for three years, when our own courts were re-established, and he was tried, sentenced, and hanged.

On another occasion I had to insist upon two of my own negroes being sent off the place, as they had been caught stealing rice. No one would try them, and my agent proposed to let them off for the present, as he nee'.ed their labour just then.

Finding things so unsettled and unsatisfactory, I determined to remain at the South during the summer, fearing that we might after all lose the crops we had with so much difficulty got planted ; and part of the hot weather I passed at St. Simon's, and part in

South Carolina, with the same friends I had been with the winter before.

On St. Simon's I found as usual a very different state of things from that on Butler's Island. The people were working like machinery, and gave no trouble at all, which was owing perhaps somewhat to the fact that there were only fifty, instead of three hundred, and at the head of the fifty was Bram, with eight of his family at work under him. He was really a remarkable man, and gave the tone to the whole place. And oh! the place was so beautiful; each day it seemed to me to grow more so. All the cattle had come down, and it was a pretty sight to see first the thirty cows, then the sheep, of which there were over a hundred, with their lambs, come in for the night, and then the horses led out to water before going to bed. I used to go round every evening to visit them in their different pens and places, where they were all put up for the night. The stable I visited several times a day, as I had not much faith in my groom, and once when I was telling him how to rub one of the horses down with a wisp of straw when he came in hot, he said, 'Yis, so my ole missus (my mother) taught me, and stand dere to see it done.' To which I could only say, 'You seem to have forgotten the lesson pretty thoroughly.'

In July I went to South Carolina, and found my friends moved from the rice plantation to a settlement about fifteen miles distant in the pine woods, which formerly had been occupied entirely by the overseers, when the gentlemen and their families could afford to spend their summer at the North, a thing they no longer could afford, nor wished to do. The place and the way of living were altogether queerer than anything I had ever imagined. The village consisted of about a dozen houses, set down here and there among the tall pine trees, which grew up to the very doors, almost hiding one house from another. The place was very healthy and the sanitary laws very strict. No two houses were allowed to be built in a line, no one was allowed to turn up the soil, even for a garden, and no one, on pain of death, to cut down a pine tree ; in which way they succeeded in keeping it perfectly free from malaria, and the air one breathed was full of the delicious fragrance of the pines, which in itself is considered a cure for most ills. In front of each house was a high mound of sand, on which at night a blazing pine fire was lit to drive away malaria that might come from the dampness of the night. These fires had the most picturesque effect, throwing their glare upon the red trunks of the pines and lighting the woods for some distance around.

The houses were built in the roughest possible manner, many of them being mere log-houses. The one we were in was neither plastered nor lined inside, one thickness of boards doing for both inside and outside walls. M—— and I slept literally under the shingles, between which and the walls of the house, we could lie and watch the stars ; but I liked feeling the soft air on my face, and to hear it sigh softly through the tall pines outside, as I lay in bed. Occasionally bats came in, which was not so pleasant, and there was not one room in the house from which you could not freely discourse with anyone in any other part of the building. Hampton Point, which I had always regarded as the roughest specimen of a house anyone could live in, was a palace compared with this. We were nevertheless perfectly comfortable, and it was really pretty, with numbers of easy-chairs and comfortable sofas about, and the pretty bright chintz curtains and covers, which looked very well against the fresh whitewashed boards ; and there was an amusing incongruity between a grand piano and fine embroidered sheets and pillow cases, relics of past days of wealth and luxury, and our bare floors and walls.

Most of the people were very poor, which

created a sort of commonwealth, as there was a friendly feeling among them all, and desire to share anything good which one got with his neighbours; so that, constantly through the day, negro servants would be seen going about from one house to another, carrying a neatly covered tray, which contained presents of cakes or fruit, or even fresh bread that some one had been baking. There was a meat club, which everyone belonged to, and to which everyone contributed in turn, either an ox or a sheep a week, which was then divided equally, each house receiving in turn a different part, so that all fared alike, and one week we feasted sumptuously off the sirloin, and the next, not so well, from the brisket.

Mrs. P—— was most energetic, directing the affairs of the estate with a masterly hand, and at the same time devoting herself to the comfort and happiness of her children; reading French or German, or practising music with her daughter in the

mornings, and being always ready to receive her boys on their return from their
hard day's work on the plantation, to which
they rode fifteen miles every morning, and
back the same distance in the evening, with
interest and sympathy in the day's work, and
a capital good dinner, which especially excited my admiration, as half the time there
really seemed nothing to make it of. But
they were better off than most of the people,
who were very wretched. Many of them had
their fine plantation houses, with everything
in them, burnt to the ground during the war,
and had no money and very little idea of
how to help themselves. In the next house
to us was Mrs. M——, an elegant, refined,
and cultivated old lady, with soft silver
grey hair and delicate features that made
her look like a picture on Sèvres china,
and as unable as a Sèvres cup to bear any
rough handling, but who lived without many
of the ordinary necessaries of life, and was
really starving to death because she could

not eat the coarse food which was all she could get.

Poor people! they were little used to such hardships, and seemed as helpless as children, but nevertheless were patient and never complained.

The woods around were full of deer, and the gentlemen hunted very often—not for sport so much as for food. They generally started about five o'clock in the morning and were aroused by a horn which was sounded in the centre of the village by the huntsman. As soon as it was heard, the hounds began to bay from the different houses, at each of which two or three were kept, no one being rich enough to keep the whole pack; but being always used to hunt together, they did very well, and made altogether a very respectable pack. One day they brought home three deer, having started ten; so for the next few days we had a grand feast of venison.

Among other subjects connected with

our rice plantations was one which interested
us all very much at that time—the question of introducing Chinese labour on our
plantations in the place of negro labour,
which just then seemed to have become
hopelessly unmanageable. There seemed
to be a general move in this direction all
through the Southern States, and I have
no doubt was only prevented by the want
of means of the planters, which, as far as
I personally am concerned, I am glad was the
case. Just then, however, we were all very
keen about it, and it sounded very easy,
the Pacific Railway having opened a way for
them to reach us. One agent actually came
for orders, and I, with the others, engaged
some seventy to try the experiment with,
first on General's Island. I confess I felt a
little nervous about the result, but agreed
with my neighbours in not being willing to
see half my property uncultivated and going
to ruin for want of labour. It was not only
that negro labour could no longer be de-

pended upon, but they seemed to be dying out so fast, that soon there would be but few left to work. This new labour would of course have sealed their doom, and in a few years none would have been left. I wrote about it at the time :—

'Poor people! it seems impossible to arouse them to any good ambition, their one idea and desire being—not to work. Their newspaper in Charlestown, edited by a negro, published an article the other day on the prospect, and said it would be the best thing that could happen to the negroes if the Chinese did come, as then they too could get them as servants, and no longer have to work even for themselves. I confess I am utterly unable to understand them, and what God's will is concerning them, unless He intended they should be slaves. This may shock you ; but why in their own country have they no past history, no monuments, no literature, never advance or improve, and here, now that they are free, are going steadily backwards, morally, intellectually, and physically. I see it on my own place, where, in spite of school and ministers, and every inducement offered them to improve their condition, they are steadily going downwards, working less and worse every year, until, from having come to them with my heart full of affection and pity for them, I am fast growing weary and disgusted.

' Mrs. P——, who when she first married and came to the South was a strong abolitionist, an intimate friend of Charles Summers and believer in Mrs. Stowe, says that she firmly believes them incapable of being raised now ; and a few days ago I had a long talk with Mrs. W——, the cousin of an Englishwoman who married and came out here with all the English horror of, and ideas about, slavery. Her husband dying shortly after, left her independent and very rich, so she determined to devote her life and means to the people who were thus thrown on her for help and protection. She first sent out to England for a young English clergyman, whom she established on the place; she then built a beautiful little church of stone, with coloured glass windows, at great expense; and their own houses, Mrs. W—— told me, were far better than English labourers' cottages.

'Well, for forty years she and her clergyman worked together among them. She never allowed one to be sold from the estate, and devoted herself to them as if they were her children. Then came the war, and in no part of the country did the negroes behave so badly as hers. They murdered the overseer, tore down the church, set up as a goddess a negro woman whom they called 'Jane Christ,' and now are in all respects as entire heathens as if they had never heard God's name mentioned, worshipping Obi, preaching every sort of heathen superstition, and a terror to the neighbourhood.[1] Mrs. W——, brokenhearted, returned to England, where she had property, and the clergyman, a Mr. G——,

---

[1] I now doubt a good deal of this story (1881).

her fellow-worker, on being asked some time ago to go to some gentleman's plantations to preach to the negroes, shook his head, and with his eyes full of tears said he would never preach again, his whole work and preaching for forty years having proved such a failure. And our own clergyman at Darien told me he had been working among the negroes all his life to the best of his powers, but felt now that not one seed sown among them had borne any good fruit.

'I confess thinking of these things makes me heartsick. I don't understand why really good men doing God's work should have failed so utterly, because although, intellectually, I feel sure the negroes are incapable of any high degree of improvement, morally, I have always thought their standard wonderfully high, considering their ignorance.'

I remained at the South until the harvest was well under way, my own interest being intensified by my friends, and we lived in a perpetual state of excitement, fearing from day to day that something would happen to destroy our hardly-made crops. First it blew hard and we feared a gale, and then the rice birds appeared in such swarms we feared the crops would be eaten up. Then it rained, and we feared the cut rice would be wetted and sprout. And so on, until one day Mrs. P—— exclaimed, 'What a state of excitement and alternate hope and fear we live in ! Why, the life of a gambler is nothing to it.' The news that reached me of the rice from Butler's Island was sufficiently good to re-assure me, but from St. Simon's it was terrible. Major D—— wrote me that the caterpillars had again attacked the cotton, and that for the third time we should probably see the entire crop eaten up before our eyes, within three weeks of perfection. Such beautiful crops as they were, too! This gave the deathblow to the Sea Island cotton, at least as far as I was concerned, for I had not capital enough to plant again after losing three crops, and the place has never been planted since, but is rented out to the negroes for a mere nominal rent, and they keep the weeds down and that is about all. Some day I hope to see it turned into a stock farm, for which it is admirably suited, and would pay well.

Before leaving the history of the South for this year, I cannot help saying a few words upon a subject which did not strike me as strange then, but does now, in looking back, as very significant of the way politics were regarded and treated by Southerners at the time. There I was, in South Carolina, 'the hot-bed of Secession,' among some of the oldest South Carolina families, considered by most Northern people as the deepest-dyed rebels, whose time was still spent in devising schemes to overthrow the Government, who therefore could not be trusted with the rights of free citizens, and whose negroes it was necessary to protect in their rights by Northern troops, and yet neither in my letters nor in my memory can I find one single instance of political discussion, or attempts to rebel against the new state of things, or desire to interfere with the new rights of the negroes. Night after night gentlemen met at one house or another, and talked and discussed one, and only one subject, and that was rice, rice, rice.

Farmers are supposed never to exhaust the two subjects of weather and the crops, and we certainly never did, until one evening the daughter of the lady with whom I was staying burst out with, 'Do—do talk of something else; I am so tired of rice, rice, from morning till night, and day after day.' We might all have been aliens and foreigners, so little interest did we any of us take in any public questions, and I never heard it suggested to prevent the negroes voting, but only to get rid of them and get reliable labour in their place. The war was over, the negroes free, and voters, and the South conquered; and never by the smallest word did I hear any suggestions made to try to alter the new condition of things, or to wish to do so, each man's motto being 'Sauve qui peut.'

CHAPTER V.

1870.

UNDER WAY.

LATE in the winter of 1869 I returned to the South, having quite made up my mind that I must change my agent. The expenses were enormous ; so large, that even remarkably good crops could not make the two ends meet, while there were no improvements made and no work done to justify such heavy expenditure, and not even accounts to show on what the money had been spent. The negroes were almost in a state of mutiny, and work for another year under existing circumstances was impossible. So I got rid of one agent and engaged another, the son of a former neighbouring planter, whom I liked personally and with whom the negroes professed themselves content. But owing to the mismanagement and want of firmness on the part of his predecessor, they were in an utterly demoralised and disorganised condition. Many of them left, not to work for anyone else, but to settle on their own properties in the pine woods; and the others seemed inclined to be very troublesome. So for a time, until the effects of being paid, and Christmas, had worn off, I left them pretty much to themselves, giving the children another pretty tea and feast, which put the older ones somewhat in a good humour.

Mr. N—— certainly did not want either courage or firmness, and I was rather startled one day to have a young man named Liverpool, who had always been a troublesome subject, burst into the room in which I was sitting, and pointing to a wound in his forehead which was bleeding pretty freely, say, ' Missus, do you allow this kind of treatment ? '

I smothered my exclamation of horror and indignant denial, and said, 'How did it happen?' 'Why,' replied the lad, 'Mr. N—— knocked me down and cut my head like this.' 'Well,' I said, 'before I decide, I must know what you have done.' 'Very well,' he said, 'very well;' and turning on his heel, left the room. I was horribly frightened for fear, in his anger, he would shoot my agent, and throwing on my shawl, I ran out to find him and put him on his guard. He told me that Liverpool had been very insolent and insubordinate to both the negro captain, who reported him, and to himself, and he had simply knocked him down, and cut his head slightly. My fears were, I believe, needless, for Liverpool's revenge was to try to sue Mr. N—— for damages, which however never came to anything, and so the trouble ended, although the man was of course dismissed from the place, being a really troublesome, bad fellow.

One of my captains also had his head cut

open by another lad who was drunk, and
who was flourishing a rice-hook about, which
the old man tried to get from him, and
was cut badly across the forehead. He came
to me to have it plastered up, and was
very anxious to know 'whether de brain
was cut,' which I assured him was not the
case, and being only a flesh wound it soon
healed.

By degrees things settled down, and the
work began. My school seemed flourishing
under a new teacher I had got from the North
(the other young man having left). This was a
young negro, who had been at a Theological
Seminary near Philadelphia, preparing himself for the ministry; but his old father, a
Massachusetts Baptist preacher, not wishing
his son to become an episcopal minister,
refused to give him any more money to con-
tinue his studies, and so he was obliged to
leave, and was anxious to get some employment by which he could earn enough money
to finish his studies. This story the Bishop

told me, adding that if I could get him some theological books, and let him read with some clergyman in the village, he would lose no time and could take up the course at the school again just where he had been obliged to leave off. Much interested, I at once got him several theological standard works which he asked for, and made arrangements with our Darien clergyman to let him read with him. How it ended belongs to next year's history. He certainly got the children on in a wonderful way ; but seeing how soon they forgot all he taught them, I doubt its having been more than a quick parrot-like manner of repeating what they had heard once or twice, which the negroes all have. But it sounded very startling to hear them rattle off the names of countries, lengths of rivers, and heights of mountains, as well as complicated answers in arithmetic. The little ones he taught to sing everything they learned, and they always began with a little song, that amused me very much, about the necessity

of coming to school and learning, the chorus
of which ran :—

> For we must get an education
> Befitting to our station
> In the rising generation
> Of the old Georg—i—ā :

a thing I fear, however, they failed to do.
One day I heard one boy say to another,
'Carolina, can you spell "going in"?' 'Gwine
in,' promptly replied Carolina, that being
their negro way of pronouncing it. On one
point I and this teacher never agreed, and
that was about the head handkerchiefs and
bead necklaces of the girls. About the last
perhaps he was right, although their love of
coloured beads was a very harmless little bit
of vanity, and I always used to give them the
handsomest I could find for their Christmas
presents ; but the head handkerchief was not
only pretty and becoming, but made them
look far neater than either their uncovered
woolly heads, or the absurd little hats they
bought and stuck on in order to follow the

fashions of their white sisters. Now that
ladies everywhere have taken to wearing
silk handkerchiefs made into turban-shaped
caps, I suppose the negro women may become reconciled to their gay bandanas.

We had a great many marriages this
winter, and wishing to encourage the girls to
become moral and chaste, we made the cere·
mony as important as possible, that is, if a
grand cake and white wreath and veil could
make it so, for the ceremony, as performed
by our old black minister, could hardly be
said to be imposing, and I think I have gone
through more painful agonies to keep from
laughing at some of these weddings than
from any physical suffering I ever experienced. The girls were always dressed in
white, with our present of the wreath and
veil to finish the costume, and the brides-
maids in white or light dresses, while the
bridegroom and groomsmen wore black frock
coats, with white waistcoats and white gloves,
all looking as nice as possible. The parson,

old John, received them at the reading-desk
of the little church, and after much arranging
of the candles, his book, and his big-rimmed
specs, would proceed and read the marriage
service of the Episcopal Church, part of which
he knew by heart, part of which he guessed
at, and the rest of which he spelt out with
much difficulty and many absurd mistakes.
Not satisfied with the usual text appointed
for the minister to read, he usually went
through all the directions too, explaining
them as he went along thus : ' " Here the man
shall take the woman by the right hand," ' at
which he would pause, look up over his
spectacles and say, ' Take her, child, by de
right hand and hold her,' and would then
proceed. On one occasion, after he had read
the sentence, ' " Whereof this ring is given
and received as a token and pledge," ' he
said with much emphasis, ' Yes, children, it
is a *plague*, but you must have patience.'
When it was all over he would say to the
bridegroom with great solemnity and a wave

of his hand, 'Salute de bride,' upon which the happy man would give her a kiss that could be heard all over the room. The worst of John's readings and explanations was that they differed every time; so we never could be prepared for what was coming, which made it all the more difficult not to laugh.

On one occasion something happened which made the people titter,—not what he said, for that was always received most reverently, but some mistake on the part of the bridegroom, upon which he closed the book and in a severe tone said, 'What you larf for? dis not trifling, dis business;' which admonition effectually sobered us all. Poor old John Bull—he was a good old man, and had an excellent influence over the people, who obeyed him implicitly, and I was really sorry when he was no longer allowed to perform the service. The Government passed a law that no unlicensed minister or magistrate could perform the marriage service, which, of course, was quite right; but not wishing to lose my parson, or to have my people go off the place to be married, I sent him up to Savannah to have him licensed. But they found him too ignorant, and refused to do so, which I dare say was quite right too ; but it spoilt all my weddings and obliged John to retire into private life.

The negroes had their own ideas of morality, and held to them very strictly ; they did not consider it wrong for a girl to have a child before she married, but afterwards were extremely severe upon anything like infidelity on her part. Indeed, the good old law of female submission to the husband's will on all points held good, and I once found a woman sitting on the church steps, rocking herself backwards and forwards in great distress, and on inquiring the cause I was told she had been turned out of church because she refused to obey her husband in a small matter. So I had to intercede for her, and on making a public apology before the whole congregation she was re-admitted.

To raise the tone among our young un-
married women was our great object, and my
friend and I dwelt much on this in teaching
them, and encouraged their marrying young,
in which, indeed, they did not need much
encouragement, for they both marry very
young, and as often as they are left widows.
The funeral service was generally performed
about three weeks after the person was buried,
in order to have a larger gathering than was
possible to get together on a short notice,
and on one occasion I was rather startled to
hear a man's second engagement announced
on the day of his first wife's funeral. The
following morning he came to me, and with
many blushes and much stammering said,
' Missus, I'se come to tell you something.'
Not choosing to acknowledge that I had
heard the gossip, I said, ' Well, Quash, what
is it?' After a very long pause and much
hesitation, he informed me he was going to be
married again. ' Don't you think it is rather
soon after Betsy's death, Quash?' I asked;

upon which he replied, 'Well, yes, missus, it is, but I thought if I waited, maybe I not get a gal suit me so well as Lizzie.' This was so unanswerable a reason that after consulting with my friend as to whether Quash's conduct could be countenanced under our code of morality, we agreed to allow it; and a very gay, fine wedding it was, for he being a good-looking carpenter and she a pretty house-servant and a great favourite of ours, we exerted ourselves especially to give them a grand wedding.

I had visits from several friends that year, and among others three Englishmen, one of whom was Mr. Leigh. I mention this because of rather a curious circumstance connected with his visit. The first Sunday after his arrival we sent him up to preach to the negroes, and he took for his text, 'And Philip said to the eunuch, Understandest thou what thou readest?' telling them that the eunuch was some Ethiopian, and was the first individual conversion to Christianity mentioned in the Bible. After church, one of the negroes came up to him and, after thanking him, said Philip was come again to the Ethiopians ; and another, called Commodore Bob, told him he had been expecting him for three weeks. And when Mr. Leigh said, 'You never saw me before, how did you know I was coming?' replied, 'Oh yes, sir, I saw you in de spirit. A milk-white gentleman rise out of the wild rushes and came and preached to us, and I said to my wife, "Katie, der will be a great movement in our church on dis Island." So I knew you in the spirit.' Of course when I told the negroes afterwards I was going to marry Mr. Leigh, old Commodore Bob was more convinced than ever that the mantle of prophecy had fallen upon his shoulders, and that the 'great movement' was my marriage to their preacher.

While I was receiving guests, and marrying and giving in marriage, the work on the plantation was going on pretty smoothly.

After the first of the year, when about twenty of the hands left, and frightened me with the idea that all were going, then the exodus stopped, and after several attempts to get the upper hand of Mr. N——, my new agent, they gave in and settled down to work. But, of course, the loss of time and hands obliged us to cut down the quantity of land planted about one-third, and the idea that each year was to begin in this way was not encouraging. So we still talked of Chinese labour and machinery (my dream just then was a steam plough which was to accomplish everything), the want of capital being our only difficulty. I adopted a new plan with the negroes this year too, and would see and speak to no one but the head men, and if anyone still insisted on coming to me directly with complaints, I simply told him he might leave the place, finding that this silenced them, but did not make them leave one whit more than when I tried to persuade them to stay.

Just before we left we had a narrow

escape from drowning, and I have always
believed that I owed my life to the presence
of mind and coolness of the negroes. We had
gone down to the cotton place to pay a farewell visit, and in coming back, crossing the
Sound, which one is obliged to do for about
five miles, we were caught in a furious gale
and cross sea. Our boat, being cut out of one
log—a regular 'dug out'—did not rise the
least to the waves, and was made doubly
heavy by having all our trunks piled in the
bow. Then, besides the four oarsmen, there
was my maid, my friend, and her sister, a
little girl of fourteen, and lastly, in the stern
steering, myself. The sea was running so high
that the boat would hardly mind the rudder
at all, and suddenly the tiller rope broke,
and I was just in time to catch the rudder
with my hand to keep it from swinging round,
and holding it so I had to steer the rest of
the way.

Not being used to steering in a rough
sea, I did not understand that the right thing

to do was to head the boat right at the waves, and could not help instinctively trying to dodge them, so that they struck us on the side and deluged us with wet besides very nearly capsizing us, and we were soon ankle deep in water. The negroes rowed with might and main, but seemed to make no progress, and the wind was blowing such a gale they could not hear me when I shouted to them at the top of my voice. About half-way across the Sound some large piles or booms had been driven during the war to prevent the Northern gunboats entering, and on these we were rapidly being driven, and I, powerless to steer against the furious wind, felt sure a few moments more would dash us against them, and we should be drowned. I in vain shouted to the men, who of course, sitting with their backs to the bow, did not see what was before them, but my voice could not reach them, so I shut my eyes and held my breath, expecting each moment to feel the blow that would send us into eternity. Just as we were literally on the piles, a huge wave struck us and drove the boat a little to one side, so that instead of striking the booms with our bow we slid between two of them, scraping each side of the boat as we did so— but were safe! Utterly exhausted, I felt I could hold on to my helm no longer, and I told my friend, who was sitting directly in front of me, to pass the order on to the men to let us drift into the marsh, where we would lie until sunset, when perhaps the wind would go down. So we beat across and reached the marsh, where we rested for a few moments, holding on by the tall rushes, but found even there the wind and waves so violent we could not remain.

The stroke oar, a man I was particularly fond of, though he was rather morose and suspicious, stood up, and holding on to the land by burying his oar in the mud, said, ' Missus, we can't stay here, the boat will be overturned. Trust me, and I will take you home safely. Only keep the head of the boat right at the waves, and don't let them strike us sideways.' So bracing myself up I took hold of my helm again, to do which I was obliged to stretch my arm as far back as possible, having no tiller rope, and we turned our head to the waves once more. The men started a favourite hymn of mine as they began to row, but the wind of heaven soon knocked the wind out of them, and they were not only obliged to stop singing, but before long were absolutely groaning at each stroke they made with the oars. Peter's speech and the attempt at a song had, however, quieted me, and enabled me to recover my presence of mind, so I kept the boat headed steadily straight at the waves, and after four hours' more hard work we landed safe on Butler's Island, the river even there being lashed into such fury by the gale that we found it difficult to get out of the boat.

The agent and negroes were terrified at the mere idea of our having attempted to cross the Sound in such weather, and advised

me, as I valued my life, not to do it again,
which was certainly a needless piece of advice.
We afterwards compared notes, my friend
saying, like a true soldier's daughter, that she
felt sure we should be drowned, and had
made up her mind to it; the little sister had
only thought it very disagreeable, and had
not known there was any danger. And my
maid said that when the first wave came she
thought of her new bonnet, and put up her
arm to save it (a very hopeless protection);
that then, when she had seen we were rushing
on the pilings, she had felt sure we should
be drowned and was very much frightened.
Still she thought of us, and said to herself,
'Well, if we are drowned, there will be far
more to mourn them than me,' which we
thought rather touching. On one point we
all agreed, and that was that the effort the
men had made to sing was done to reassure
me; and as a proof of how exhausted they were
with their work, when I sent up for them,
not an hour after our arrival on the Island, to

give them some whisky, they were all lying
on the floor before the fire, sound asleep.
My arm, with which I had held the helm,
ached and trembled so for four days afterwards that I could not use it; but thank God
we were safe, and in less than a week afterwards on our way to the North.

A month later I went to England with
my sister, hoping things would work smoothly
enough at the South to enable me to stay
abroad all winter. . . . Vain hope!

CHAPTER VI.

FRESH DIFFICULTIES—NEGRO TRAITS—

ABDICATION.

IN December I returned to the United States
and the South, the reports I had received
of the condition of things during my absence
not being satisfactory, and they certainly did
not improve on closer examination. There
were no accounts at all at this time, but much
money spent, and what my agent had done
to set things so by the ears I never could
make out, but by the ears they undeniably
were. He had been very injudicious, and
was far too hot-tempered to manage any
people. The whole plantation was up in
arms; half the people had gone and the other
half were ready to go when I arrived, and it
was desperately hard work to restore any-

thing like order. Even as late as the end of
January I thought I should have to give up
all idea of planting the larger Island. I merely
put in about two hundred acres on General's
Island, but by dint of bullying, scolding, and
a little judicious compromising, I kept those
who were going and brought back some who
had left. One man, who had been a favourite
of mine, tried to get off without seeing me ;
but, hearing he was going, I went up to his
house and asked him what he was about, to
which he replied, ' Moving, missus, but I did
not mean to let you catch me ; ' to which I
said, ' Well, I have caught you, and you can
just stop moving, for I don't intend you to
leave the place,' which settled him, and he
has been ploughing now steadily for three
days. To-night the last man came in, and
told me he would go to work in the morning.
So now the machine is fairly started again,
and will run for the year, the getting off being
the only difficulty.

I was very unhappy about my stroke oar,

Peter Mack, who behaved so splendidly last
spring in that gale on the Sound, and who
had also made up his mind to leave. I did
not say one word to him, thinking that the
best course to pursue in his case ; but when
yesterday he came in to report himself ready
for work, I said, ' Well, Peter, I am glad you
are going to stay. I was sorry to hear you
were so anxious to leave me.' ' No, missus,'
he said, ' I not so anxious to leave you, else I
done gone, but if you had not come I should
have gone.' This being obliged to use
personal influence in every individual case
was rather troublesome, and yet it was very
pleasant to have them affectionate in their
manner to me, and influenced by my presence
into doing what I wanted.

Not being able at once to find anyone
in Mr. N——'s place, I determined to try
working with the negro captains alone, and
endeavoured to excite their ambition and
pride by telling them that everything depended upon them now, and I expected them

to show me how well they could manage, and what a fine crop they would raise for me. My friend Major D——, who, after six years of failure at cotton-planting had determined to give it up, but was anxious to remain at the South, consented to take charge of the financial part of the work for me, which was a great relief to my mind, and things seemed really for a time as if they would work smoothly.

My school arrangements were not going well at all, and I soon found that the teacher I had was a very different person from what I had hoped and believed him to be. He also had got bitten with the political mania, and asked my permission to accept some small office in Darien, assessor of taxes I think it was, which would not in any way interfere with his work for me, but greatly increase his income. So I could not well refuse, although I did not like it, and it was on my first return that he asked me, before I had found out other things about him. I after-

wards found that he had entirely given up
teaching Sunday school, or holding any
services for the people on Sunday, and when
I asked him why, merely said the people and
children would not attend ; then, that he had
quite given up all attempts at carrying on
his own studies, and was no longer reading
divinity with our Darien clergyman, but
instead, was mixing himself up with all the
local Darien politics ; and, lastly, bore but a
very indifferent character there for morality,
which at first I was inclined to disbelieve,
until a disastrous affair proved the correctness
of the reports. But this did not happen till
the following year.

Either I am right in believing the negro
incapable of any high degree of intellectual
training, or of being raised to a position of
equality with the white race without deterio-
rating morally, or my experience has been
very unfortunate. This man was one proof
of it, another was a negro clergyman, born in
one of the British Colonies, educated in an

English college, and ordained deacon by an
English Colonial bishop, so that never at any
period of his life was he affected by having
been a slave or held an inferior position. He
had a church in Savannah, and conducted
the service as he had been used to hearing it
done, which was chorally; he had a fine
voice, and chanted and intoned very well
himself, and had trained a choir of little
negroes, whom he put in surplices, extremely
well. I was much interested in all the
accounts I had heard of him, and when I
reached Savannah I went to his church, believing that at last my question of whether
a full-blooded negro was capable of moral
and intellectual elevation, was affirmatively
answered. A full-blooded African he certainly was, and was so black you could hardly
see him. The service was beautifully done,
and his part of it was well and effectively
rendered, so that I was wrought up to the
highest pitch of excitement and enthusiasm
when the sermon came, for which I had been

anxiously waiting. It was on a religious life, and from beginning to end was highflown, and mere fine talk ; and when he mentioned the 'infidel Voltaire and the licentious Earl of Rochester' (his audience being composed, with the exception of my friend and myself, of the most ignorant and simple negroes), my enthusiasm and excitement collapsed with a crash, and I could have cried with grief and disappointment. Here were just the same old predominating negro traits—vanity, conceit, and love of showing off. About that man, too, there were stories told very unbecoming a clergyman, and though I believe none of them were ever directly proved, he lost caste generally, and later on left Savannah.

Another instance of disappointment was the son of one of our own head men, whom my sister and myself tried to have educated at the North, hoping he might become a teacher on the Island. His father is one of the best, most intelligent, and trustworthy

men I ever knew, and with much more firmness of character than the negroes generally
possess, so much so that being now our head
man he controls everything, and the gang of
Irishmen who come to us regularly every
winter obey his orders and work under him
with perfect good temper and willingness—the
only case of the sort I know ; and this man
can neither read nor write, and is totally
ignorant about everything but his work.
He comes of a good stock ; his great-grandfather was my great-grandfather's foreman,
and of his uncle, who died in 1866, my
father, then alive, writes as follows : ' It is
with very sad feelings that I write to tell
you of the death of Morris, the head man
of General's Island ; he was attacked with
fever, and died in four days. Dr. Kenan
attended him and I nursed him, but his
disease was malignant in its character, and
the medicines produced no effect. To me
his loss is irreparable ; he was by far the
most intellectual negro I have ever known

among our slaves. His sense and judgment
were those of the white race rather than the
black, and the view he took of the present
position of his race was sensible and correct.
He knew that freedom entailed self-depend-
ence and labour, not idleness, and he set an
example to those whose labours he directed
by never sparing himself in any way where
work was to be done. These qualities were
inherited ; his grandfather, likewise named
Morris, was my grandfather's driver, and on
one occasion was working on that exposed
cotton tract situated on the small island
opposite St. Simon's, and in consequence of
the situation being so much exposed to the
autumn gales, which are often tropical in
their fury, no settlement was ever made on
this tract, the negroes who worked it going
over daily in boats from their houses on St.
Simon's. The only building was the hurricane house, which was constructed of sufficient strength to withstand the force of the
gales, and in one of the years—1804 I think

it was—when a terrific gale visited the coast
and the negroes were at work on this place,
old Morris, seeing signs of an approaching storm, ordered the people into that hurricane house.   They, not wishing to take
refuge there, preferred to make the attempt
of reaching St. Simon's before the storm
burst ; but old Morris, knowing that there
was no time for this, drove them with the
lash into the house, where they were hardly
secured when the storm broke, and turned
out to be one of the most terrible ever known
on the southern coast.   Of our negroes not
a life was lost, though upwards of a hundred
were drowned from a neighbouring island,
who had rushed into their boats and tried to
reach the mainland.   My grandfather, wishing to reward Morris for his praiseworthy
conduct, offered him his freedom, which,
however, he declined, as he had a wife and
family on the island, and preferred remaining.
My grandfather then presented him with a
considerable sum of money and a silver

goblet, on which was engraved the following
inscription :—

TO MORRIS,

FROM

P. BUTLER,

For his faithful, judicious, and spirited conduct in
the hurricane of September 8, 1804, whereby
the lives of more than 100 persons were,
by Divine permission, saved.

'This passed to his son, also a superior
man, and from him to his grandson, Morris,
who possessed it at the time of his death.
He left no son to succeed him, but his
nephew, Sey, I think, promises to turn out
a worthy descendant.'

This man, Sey, quite fulfilled my father's
expectations, and was soon placed in a
position of trust, from which he rose to be
my foreman, the post he now holds. My
sister and myself thought, therefore, that we
could not do better than choose his son to
be educated as a teacher, hoping that he
would inherit his father's good qualities,
moral and intellectual, and being glad to

show our appreciation of his father in this way. We accordingly sent him to a large negro school or college in Philadelphia, which was under the direction of the Quakers, and in every way admirably managed, except that unless all the students were instructed for teachers, the course of education, which comprised Greek and Latin, algebra and trigonometry, was rather unsuited to fit them for any manual labour by which they might have to earn their bread. But this fault would apply to all American schools, I think, of this order. We made arrangements that little Abraham should lodge with the lady superintendent of the school, and nothing could have been more promising or more satisfactory than his start.

For the first six months or year every-thing went well, and he learnt fast. Then the reports became less and less satisfactory, until, at the end of the second year, we were requested to remove him, as he was incor-rigibly bad—had broken open the teacher's desk, and climbed over the wall and in at the window of the school-house to steal, and otherwise so misbehaved himself as to make it impossible for them to keep him. I was dreadfully sorry to have to break this news to Sey, and I told him as gently as I could, but he felt the disgrace of having his son returned to him under such circumstances most keenly.

The lad returned to the plantation, and his father at once set him to work in the field; but time after time he ran off, twice stealing his father's money, until at last Sey begged that his name might be struck from off the books, as he himself would no longer have anything to do with him. Of course I don't pretend to say that having him educated was the entire cause of his turning out so badly, but I do believe that, had we never taken him from the South, and he had grown up under his father's severe and high standard of right, he would probably have turned out very differently. I think most likely that he was taught and encouraged in his bad ways by the town boys, who, finding him on his first arrival a simple and easy tool to manage, made a cat's-paw of him ; for, as I told his teacher, he certainly did not learn to climb walls and break in windows on the plantation, for there were no walls to climb or windows to break open there.

Last winter, when my husband returned to the South for a short time, he found Abraham there again, at work under his father once more, having been to the North and elsewhere to look for work, but without success. I fear, however, that he was not much improved, from a story my husband told me of him. He said he was standing near the mill one day, where all the people were at work, when he saw several of the negroes running towards him, crying out, ' Crazy man !' ' crazy man !' and perceived that Abraham—now grown into a powerful, large man—was rushing after them, brandishing an axe. He was followed by his father, who was trying to disarm him, but whenever he approached near, Abraham threatened to brain him, so Sey could not get at him. He rushed past Mr. Leigh and into the mill, where the terrified women and children at work scattered in all directions ; then, going out on the wharf and throwing his arms up, made a tragical speech and prepared to jump into the river. This my husband at once called to his father and the others to let him do, and when he had taken the wild plunge, had him pulled into a boat, brought in, rubbed down, put to bed, and left to recover, which he did after a long sleep, being apparently quite well the next day. Sey's explanation was that he had trouble in his head, and had been like this before ; but whether he really did not know, or was ashamed to confess, that his son had been drinking, I do not know, but I believe that was undoubtedly the case.

There was another half-descendant of old Morris—a son of a daughter of his by a white man whom she had met while in the interior during the war. Whatever became of the father is not known, as is usually the case in such instances, and the mother dying before the end of the war, old Morris took the little boy and his sister (whose father had undoubtedly been black, for she was as black as a little coal, while Dan, the boy, showed his white blood very plainly, and was extremely pretty), and it was with Morris's widow, old Cinda, that I found the two children living when I first took charge of the place, my father having allowed all three rations. My husband, who opened a night school the first year of our return after our marriage, soon picked Dan out as a favourite and begged me to give him employment about the house, which I did. I then took him to the North for the summer, and finally brought him to England. Having when I first married brought over a negro servant who gave me a good deal of trouble, although perhaps he was hardly to be blamed for having his head turned, considering how much all the English maid-servants preferred him to a white man, and that my lady's maid finally preferred to marry him—a penchant I could neither understand nor sympathise with—I had declared I would never bring another negro over; but the desire to have one of my own people about me, Dan's youth, and my fondness for the boy, prevailed, and I brought him. He was made the greatest pet by everyone—his pretty face, gentle voice, and extreme civility making everyone his friend. The butlers at all the large houses I took him to said he was worth a dozen white boys. My own cook, who was old enough to be his mother, kept all the tit-bits and nice morsels for him, all the women servants spoilt and petted him, and I foresaw that very soon he would be utterly ruined, as no one kept him up to his work, and everyone let him do pretty much as he pleased.

I was therefore greatly surprised to have

him come to me one day and say he wished
to be sent home, as he did not like his life in
England ; the work was too hard.   I had been
scolding him for some neglect of duty the
day before, and supposed he was a little put
out and would soon get over it, as his work
was certainly not hard, although it was of
course regular, a thing I am sure a negro
finds more irksome than anything else, as
they seem to require at least half the day to
lounge.   Dan, however, never altered his
desire, although I spoke to him several times
about it, and after being over two years in
England, not only well fed and clothed, but
petted and spoilt, he returned to the plantation last winter.   The boy had so much good
in him and was so clever, besides having had
such advantages, that I could not bear to let
him go back to the South just to run wild
and go to the bad, so I had a serious talk
with him before he left, and made him promise
that he would really take up some regular
trade, and as he chose carpentering, my

husband, who took him out, apprenticed him to our head carpenter, and I have hopes of his turning out well yet. But why he preferred returning to his rough and uncomfortable plantation life after having lived on the fat of the land in England, I never have understood, unless it be that the restraints of civilised life and regular habits were irksome and disagreeable to him.

Meanwhile the winter wore on, the last I was ever to spend on the place as mistress, or rather supreme dictator, whose acts had hitherto been controlled by neither master nor partner. My last letter written before leaving is as follows :—

Butler's Island : March 1871.

Dearest M——, My little place never looked so lovely, and the negroes are behaving like angels, so that my heart is very sad at the thought of leaving ; for although I suppose I shall come back some day, it will not be for some time, and no one knows what changes may take place meanwhile, and notwithstanding all the trouble I have had I do love my home and work here so dearly. I never worked so hard as I have this winter, but never has my work been so satisfactory. I wrote you in my last how well my negroes were doing under my management, and I find the news of my success has spread far and wide. Everyone on the river started before I did, yet now I am far ahead of them all, being the only planter on the river who was ready to plant on the first tides. I began to feel a little anxious, however, at the idea of leaving the place entirely in charge of the negro captains as the time for my departure drew near, and so was greatly relieved when they came to me a few weeks ago, and begged that I would leave some one over them in my place when I left, saying, ' Missus, we must have a white man to back us when you gone ; de people not mind what we say :' which is one of the many proofs of how incapable of self-government ment these people are, and how dependent upon the white race for support. I therefore looked out for an overseer to take charge of the planting (Major D—— acting only as my financial manager), and have engaged a Mr. S——, formerly an overseer at Altama, of whom both Mr. C—— and the other gentlemen on the river who know him speak very highly in every way. He has been here about a week now, and so far has got on very well with the negroes, who usually try all sorts of pranks with a new-comer to see how much they can make out of him. He told Major D—— yesterday that he was utterly surprised at the condition of the place, as never since the war had he seen one in such good order, work so well done, and so orderly, obedient, and civil a set of negroes.

Dear M——, don't laugh at my boasting. I have worked so hard and cared so much about it, that it is more to me than I can express to know that I have succeeded. Major D—— too has straightened out all the accounts, so far as he can, of the past three years, so that I now see exactly what money has been made and what spent, and although I am not quite prepared to say that anyone has cheated me, the reckless expenditure and extravagance that has been going on, with the absolute want of conscientious responsibility shown by my agents, makes me ill to think of. However, it is all over now, thank goodness ! and I can not only hope to at last make something out of the place, but leave it with a feeling of perfect security.

My people had done so well that, feeling inclined for a little amusement myself, I thought I would reward them, and so gave them a holiday one day last week, and got up a boat race between my hands and Mr. C——'s, which was great fun. The river was crowded with boats of all sizes and shapes, in the midst of which lay the two elegant little race boats, manned by six of my men and six of the Altama negroes. Splendid fellows all of them, wild with excitement and showing every tooth in their heads, they were on such a broad grin.

Major W——, who was staying with me, steered my boat, and Mr. C—— the other, Major D—— acting as starting judge, and at the crack of his pistol off they started, working like men, perfectly cool and steady, rowing down the river like the wind side by side, until they were within a few hundred feet of the wharf which was to be the goal, and on which Mr. C——, his son, Mrs. C——, Admiral T——, and F—— and I were all assembled. Then my men made a mighty effort and shot ahead, winning by about four seconds. We had two races afterwards, one of which we beat, so that out of the three we won two. It was such fun, and I wish you could have heard the negroes afterwards, ' explaining matters.'

To-day, a poor blind woman, whose eyes F—— and S—— sometimes bathe, said to me, ' Missus, when we meet in heaven, and dey say to me, Tina, der's your missus, I not look for your face, missus, for I not know dat, but I shall look for your works, as I shall know dem.' I was very much touched, indeed my heart is altogether very sad, and full of love for my poor people here, and I can't bear to think that in two weeks I shall have left them for so long. Good-bye.

Yours affectionately,

F——.

CHAPTER VII.

1871, 1872, AND 1873.

ABSENTEES—A NEW MASTER—WHITE LABOURERS
—'MASSA'—'LITTLE MISSUS'—NORTHERN
IDEAS—CHURCH WORK—GOOD-BYE.

In May of the same year I sailed for Europe,
and in June was married. I remained in
England until the autumn of 1873, when we
returned to the United States. During the
interval the accounts that reached us from the
South were not satisfactory. The expenses,
it is true, were cut down to nearly one-half
what they had been before, and the negroes
gave but little trouble, but one overseer
turned out to be very incapable and entirely
wanting in energy, making no fresh improvements and planting the same fields each
year that had been under cultivation since the

war, letting all the rest of the place grow into a complete wilderness. We also had a terrible loss during our absence in the destruction by fire of our mills and principal buildings. They were undoubtedly set on fire by one of the negroes to whom we had shown many and special favours, which had only had the effect of spoiling him to such an extent that he would not bear the slightest contradiction or fault found with his work. He had been reprimanded by the overseer and a dollar deducted from his wages for some neglect in his work, and this put him into such a passion that he refused to take his wages at all and went off, saying that it should cost us more than a dollar. This, and the fact that he was seen about the mill the morning of the fire, where he had no business to be, made us feel pretty sure that he was the incendiary, and although we never could prove it, it was a generally accepted idea that he was the man.

By this fire about fifteen thousand dollars'

worth of property was destroyed, including all our seed rice for the coming planting, and had it not been for the efforts of the Irishmen who were at work on the place, the dwelling-houses and other buildings would have gone too. The sight of a large fire seems to arouse the savage nature of the negroes ; they shout and yell and dance about like fiends, and often become possessed by an incendiary mania which results in a series of fires. They never attempt to put it out, even if it is their own property burning.

Soon after this came the news that the teacher I had left on the Island to train and educate the people, not only intellectually but morally, had turned out very badly, and had led one of my nicest young servant girls astray, which, with the other disaster, so disheartened me as to make me feel unable to struggle any longer against the fate which seemed to frustrate all my efforts either to improve the property or the condition of the people, and I said I would do no more. My husband, however, took a more practical view of the matter, and decided that as we could not abandon the property altogether we must go on working it, so he telegraphed the agent to get estimates for a new mill and to buy seed, and in fact to go on, which he did, and in course of time a new mill was built and a fresh crop planted.

In the autumn of 1873 we determined to return to America, and the agitation among the agricultural labourers in England being then at its height, I thought we might advantageously avail ourselves of the rage among them for emigration, to induce a few to go out to Butler's Island and take the place of our Irish labourers there. It seemed a capital plan, but I did not know then what poor stuff the English agricultural labourer is made of as a general rule. Eight agreed to go, and a contract was made with them for three years, by which we bound ourselves to send them back at the end of the time should they desire to come, and have in the meantime fulfilled their part of the agreement; the wages we agreed to give them were the highest given in the United States, and about three times higher than what they had received at home. As we intended to stop some little time at the North we shipped them direct to the South, where they arrived about a month before we did. On November 1 we followed, and I was most warmly greeted by all the negroes, who at once accepted my husband as ' massa.'

Our own people seemed pretty well settled, and Major D—— said gave but little trouble, the greatest improvement being in their acceptance of their wages every Saturday night without the endless disputes and arguments in which they used formerly to indulge whenever they were paid. But there were still a great many idle worthless ones hanging about Darien, and when we arrived the wharf was crowded with as dirty and demoralised a looking lot of negroes as I ever saw, and these gave the town a bad name.

Our Englishmen we found settled in the old hospital building which I had assigned to them, and which had been unoccupied since the school had been broken up, with the exception of one room which the people still used as their church. Besides this there were three others, about twenty feet square, nicely ceiled and plastered, into which I had directed the Englishmen should be put, and in *one* of these we found them all, eight men sleeping, eating, and living in the same room, from preference. They had not made the least effort to make themselves decently comfortable, and were lying upon the floor like dogs, although Major D—— had advised them to put up some bedsteads, offering the carpenter of the party lumber for the purpose, and an old negro woman to make them some straw mattresses, giving them a week to get things straight before they began their work. Two of them fell ill soon after, and then we insisted upon their dividing, half the number using one sleeping room and the rest the

other, keeping the third for a general living
room, kitchen, &c. At first they seemed in
good spirits and well satisfied, but nothing
can describe their helplessness and want of
adaptability to the new and different circumstances in which they found themselves.
They were like so many troublesome children, and bothered me extremely by coming
to the house the whole time to ask for something or other, until at last, one Saturday
evening when they came to know if I would
let them have a little coffee for Sunday, as
they had forgotten to buy any, the shop
being only half a mile distant across the
river, I flatly refused, and said they must
learn to take care of themselves. One was
afterwards very ill, and I really thought he
would die from want of heart, as from the
first moment he was taken ill he made up
his mind he should not recover, and I had
to nurse him like a baby, giving him his
medicine and food with my own hands, and
finally when he was really well, only weak,

we had to insist upon his getting up and trying to move about a little, or I think he would have spent the rest of his life in bed.

To make a long story short, they soon began to get troublesome and discontented, were constantly drunk, and shirked their work so abominably, that our negro foreman Sey begged that they might not be allowed to work in the same fields with his negroes, to whom they set so bad an example, by leaving before their day's work was finished, that they demoralised his gang completely, and made them grumble at being obliged to go on with their work after the ' white men ' had left. So when the end of their second year came we were most thankful to pay their way back to England and get rid of them.   All left except one, who after starting rather badly settled down and became a useful hard-working man, and is still with us as head ploughman, in which capacity he works for about eight months of the year, spending the other three or four on our deserted cotton place, as the unhealthiness of the rice plantation prevents his remaining there during the summer months. During this time he plants a good vegetable garden for himself, spends most of his time fishing, and is taken care of by an old negro woman, who he assured my husband worked harder and was worth more than any white woman he had ever seen. But I am afraid his experience had been unfortunate, for he was the only married man in the party we brought out, and his being the only one who did not wish to return made us suspect domestic troubles might have had something to do with his willingness to stay.

We had for several years employed a gang of Irish labourers to do the banking and ditching on the Island, and although we made no agreement with them about return-ing in the spring when we dismissed them, they came down each succeeding autumn, taking the risk of either being engaged again by us or by some of our neighbours, and

hitherto we had always been ready to do so.
But the winter we first had our Englishmen
we decided not to have the additional heavy
expense of the Irishmen, and so told them
we did not want them.   The result was that
they were very indignant with the Englishmen, whom they regarded as usurpers and
interlopers, and whose heads they threatened
to break in consequence.

Major D——, half in fun, said to them,
' Why, you shouldn't hate them ; you all come
from the same country.'   To which Pat indignantly replied, ' The same country, is it ? Ah,
thin, jist you put them in the ditch along wid
us, and ye'll soon see if it's the same country
we come from.'   A test they were quite safe
in proposing, for the Englishmen certainly
could not hold a spade to them, and after
trying the latter in the ditch we were glad
enough to engage our Irishmen again, which
quite satisfied them, so that after that they
got on very well with their ' fellow country-
men,' only occasionally indulging in a little

Irish wit at their expense. They certainly were a very different lot of men, and while the Englishmen were endless in their complaints, wants, and need of assistance, the Irishmen turned into a big barn at the upper end of the plantation, got an old negro woman to cook for them, worked well and faithfully, were perfectly satisfied, and with the exception of occasionally meeting them going home from their work of an evening when I was walking, I never should have known they were on the place.

I must record one act to their honour, for which I shall ever feel grateful. Two years after the one of which I am now writing I was very ill on the plantation, and the white woman I had taken from the North as cook was lying dangerously ill at the same time, so that the management and direction of everything fell upon my nurse, an excellent Scotchwoman, who found some difficulty in providing for all the various wants of such a sick household. The Irishmen hearing her say

P

one day that she did not know where she should get anything that I could eat, brought her down some game they had shot for themselves, and, being told that I liked it, every Monday morning regularly, for the rest of the winter, sent me in either hares, snipe, or ducks by one of the servants, without even waiting to be thanked, the game they shot being what they themselves depended upon for helping out their scanty larder.

I felt a little anxious at first about the effect such a new life and strange surroundings might have upon my husband, for although he had seen it before, it was a very different matter merely looking at it from a visitor's point of view, and returning to live there as owner, when all the differences between it and his life and home in England would be so apparent. However, I soon found that I need not be uneasy upon that score, as he at once became deeply interested in it, and set about learning all the details of the work and peculiarities of both place and

people, which he mastered in a wonderfully
short time, showing a quick appreciation of
the faults and mistakes in the previous system
of planting which he had followed since the
war, and which he very soon tried on an
entirely different plan. This was so successful that in a year the yield from the place
was doubled and the whole plantation bore a
different aspect, much to the astonishment
of our neighbours, who could not understand
how an Englishman, and English parson at
that, who had never seen a rice field before
in his life, should suddenly become such a
good planter. The negroes, after trying
what sort of stuff he was made of, became
very devoted to him, and one of the old men,
after informing my sister some little time
afterwards how much they liked him and
how much good he had done them all, wound
up with ‘Miss Fanny (me) made a good
bargain dat time.’

My husband wrote a number of letters to
England from the plantation during the time

we remained there, which were published in a little village magazine for the amusement of the parishioners who knew him, and which I think I cannot do better than add to this account of mine, as they will show how everything at the South struck the fresh and unbiassed mind of a foreigner who had no traditions, no old associations, and no prejudices, unless indeed unfavourable ones, to influence him.

After having spent the summer at the North, we again returned to the plantation in November, taking with us this time an addition to the family in the shape of a little three-months-old baby, who was received most warmly by the negroes, and christened at once 'Little Missus,' many of them telling me, with grins of delight, how they remembered me 'just so big.' I very soon found that the arrival of 'young missus' had advanced me to the questionable position of 'old missus,' to which however I soon became reconciled when I found how tenderly 'Little

Missus' was treated by all her devoted subjects. Oddly enough, the black faces never
seemed to frighten her, and from the first she
willingly went to the sable arms stretched
out to take her. It was a pretty sight to see
the black nurse, with her shining ebony face,
surmounted by her bright-coloured turban,
holding the little delicate white figure up
among the branches of the orange trees to
let her catch the golden fruit in her tiny
hands ; and the house was kept supplied
almost the whole winter with eggs and
chickens, brought as presents to ' Little
Missus.'

Another summer at the North and back
again to the South, from whence nothing but
good reports had reached us of both harvest
and people. Indeed our troubles of all sorts
seemed to be at an end, at least such as arose
from 'reconstruction.' It came in another
shape, however, and in January 1876 I was
taken very ill, and for five days lay at the
point of death, during which time the anxiety

and affection shown by my negroes was most profound, all work stopped, and the house was besieged day and night by anxious inquirers. My negro nurse lay on the floor outside my door all night, and the morning I was pronounced out of danger she rushed out, and throwing up her arms, exclaimed, ' My missus'll get well ; my missus'll get well ! I don't care what happens to me now.' And when at last I was able to get about once more, the expressions of thankfulness that greeted me on all sides were most touching. One woman, meeting me on the bank, flung herself full length on the ground, and catching me round the knees, exclaimed, ' Oh, tank de Lord, he spared my missus.' A man to whom something was owing for some chickens he had furnished to the house during my illness refused to take any money for them, saying when I wished to pay him, ' No, dey tell me de chickens was for my missus, and I'se so glad she's got well I don't want no money for dem.' My dear people !

Our poor old housekeeper, less fortunate
than myself, did not recover, but died just as
I was getting better, and in looking over her
letters after her death, in order to find out
where her friends lived, so as to let them
know of her death, I found to my astonishment that she had been in terror of the
negroes from the first, and had a perfect
horror of them. Being so fond of them myself, and feeling such entire confidence in
them as not even to lock the doors of the
house at night, it never occurred to me that
perhaps a New England woman, who had
never seen more than half-a-dozen negroes
together in her life, might be frightened at
finding herself surrounded by two or three
hundred, and it was only after her death that
I found from the letters written to her by
different friends at the North, in answer to
hers, what her state of mind had been. There
were such expressions as these : 'I don't
wonder you are frightened and think you
hear stealthy steps going about the house at

night.' ' How horrible to be on the Island
with all those dreadful blacks.' ' The idea of
there being only you three white people on
the Island with two hundred blacks!' &c.
She had apparently forgotten, in making her
statement, the eight Irish and six English
labourers who were living on the Island, but
still the negroes certainly did greatly outnumber the whites, and could easily have
murdered us all had they been so inclined.
But there was not the least danger then,
whatever there might have been the first year
or two after the war, and even at that time I
never felt afraid, for had there been a general
negro insurrection, although my own negroes
would of course have joined it, there were
at least a dozen, I am sure, who would have
warned me to leave the place in time.

My sister paid me a visit this winter—her
first to the South since the war, except in
1867, when she spent a month with us, but
on St. Simon's Island, where she saw little or
nothing of the negroes—and she was greatly

struck with their whole condition and demeanour, in which she said she could not perceive that freedom had made any difference. In answer to this I could only say that if she had been at the South the first three years after the war, she would have seen a great change in their deportment, but that since that they had gradually been coming back to their senses and 'their manners.'

This winter we had the pleasure of seeing a very nice church started in Darien for the negroes. For three years my husband had been holding services for them regularly on the Island in a large unoccupied room which we had fitted as a chapel ; but we found this hardly large enough to accommodate outsiders, and as many wished to attend who were not our own people, we thought Darien the best place for the church. While it was being built, service was held in a large barn or warehouse, which was kindly lent for the purpose by a coloured man of considerable property and good standing in the community, who although a staunch supporter of the Presbyterian Church himself, was liberal-minded enough to lend a helping hand to his brethren of a different persuasion.

The following extract from the report of our Bishop came to me somewhat later :—

April 9.—Held evening service, assisted by the Rev. J. W. Leigh, of England, and the Rev. Dr. Clute. Confirmed twenty-one coloured persons, and addressed the candidates in St. Philip's Mission Chapel, Butler's Island. I desire publicly to express my thanks to the Rev. Mr. Leigh, for the faithful and efficient service he has rendered the Church in Georgia during his stay in America. He has trained the coloured people on Butler's Island in the doctrines, and has brought to bear upon them the elevating influence, of the Church, with a thoroughness and kindness which must, under God, be fraught with good to those poor people who for so many years have been the victims of so-called religious excitements and fancied religious experiences.

April 11.—Held morning service, assisted by the Rev. Dr. Clute. Preached, and confirmed six in St. Andrew's, Darien. In the afternoon I held service for coloured people in Darien, assisted by the Rev. Dr. Clute, who presented seven coloured candidates for confirmation, and the Rev. Mr. Leigh, who presented one. After confirmation I addressed the candidates. In the evening I held service in the Methodist Church, assisted by the same brethren. Preached, and confirmed three coloured persons in Darien. The Church is taking a strong hold upon the coloured people in Darien, as also upon Butler's Island. The Rev. Dr. Clute had twenty-eight candidates whom he expected to present, but they were prevented from coming by a storm.

Also in the appendix is added the following paragraph :—

The Rev. the Hon. J. W. Leigh, M.A., reports from Butler's Island that he has had fourteen baptisms, twenty-two candidates confirmed, twenty-nine communicants, and three marriages. It is also announced that the frame of the Chapel (St. Athanasius) for the coloured mission in Darien has been erected, and will be enclosed as soon as money can be obtained for the expense. The confirmed, as well as many candidates who were absent from the rite because of a rain-storm and change of the day of appointment, have had no opportunity to communicate.

This winter was destined to be the last I was to spend at the South, as my husband had made up his mind finally to return to his own country to live. Before leaving I had broken up my little plantation establishment, selling the principal part of the furniture, carpets, and so forth, and I consider it a significant proof of the well-to-do condition of the negroes, that the best and most expensive things were bought and paid for on the spot by negroes. The drawing-room carpet, a handsome Brussels one, was bought by a rich coloured man in Darien, the owner of a large timber mill there, a man universally respected by everyone, and, if I am not mistaken, who has for years held an official position of some importance in Darien. He was not a slave before the war, but owned slaves himself.

The following November my husband returned to the plantation for a couple of months alone, in order to settle up everything finally, before we sailed in January for England. This was the winter of the Presidential election, when our part of the country was, like every other section, violently agitated and excited by politics. But with us, while of course everyone did the best he could for his party, there was not the least ill-feeling between the blacks and the whites, and the election passed off without any trouble of any sort, which is a noteworthy fact in itself, as our county is one of the two in Georgia where the negroes outnumber the whites ten to one, and in more than one instance a negro was elected to office by the white democratic votes.

CHAPTER VIII.

1877, 1878, 1879.

OVER THE WATER.

AND now I have come to these last three
years of my history, which are so much the
same, and marked by so few incidents, that a
few pages will suffice for them.

In the autumn of 1877, not a year after
our return to England, our old friend and
agent Major D—— died, and in many ways
his loss was an irreparable one to us, but
nothing showed the changed and improved
condition of the negroes more than the fact
that his death did not in the least unsettle
them, and that the work went steadily on
just the same. A few years before, a sort of

panic would have seized them, and the idea taken possession of them that a new man would not pay them, or would work them too hard, or make new rules, &c. &c., and it would have been months before we got them quieted and settled down again.   But now, although Major D—— was much liked and respected by them, as indeed he was by the whole community, Northern man though he was, and Northern soldier though he had been, they knew that whoever was put in his place would carry out the old rules, and pay them their wages as regularly as before.

In September of the year 1878 a terrible storm visited the Southern coast.   The hurricane swept over the Island just in the middle of the harvest, and quite half the crop was entirely destroyed, and the rest injured. What was saved was only rescued by the most energetic and laborious efforts on the part of the negroes, who did their utmost. Day after day they did almost double their usual task, several times working right

through the night, and twice all Sunday ;
cheerfully and willingly, not as men who
were working for wages, but as men whose
heart was in their work, and who felt their
interests to be the same as their employer's.

Later on in the same year my husband
returned to the United States and revisited
the property, but finding everything working
well and satisfactorily, only remained about
six weeks.

Our present manager is the son of a
former neighbour of ours, whom the negroes
have known from childhood, and to whose
control they willingly submit. In engaging
a person to manage such a property two
things are necessary : first, that he should be
a Southern man, because no one not brought
up with the negroes can understand their
peculiarities, and a Northern man, with every
desire to be just and kind, invariably fails
from not understanding their character.
Even Major D——— felt this, although he had
been so long among them, and latterly never

would take charge of any but the financial part of the business. And secondly, the person put over them must be a gentleman born and bred, for they have the most comical contempt for anyone they do not consider 'quite the thing,' and they perceive instinctively the difference. This I suppose is a remnant of slave times, when there were the masters, the slaves, and the poor white class, regarded with utter contempt by the negroes, who called them 'poor white trash.' To a gentleman's rule they will submit, but to no other, and it is useless to put a person holding an inferior social position over them.

The only plantations near us which are well and successfully worked, are managed either by their old masters, or gentlemen from the neighbourhood. We all pay wages either weekly or monthly, finding that the best plan now. It is far the easiest for ourselves, as well as satisfactory to the negroes, who can't think they are cheated when everything is paid in full every Saturday night,

nor can they forget in that short time what
days they have been absent or missed work.
I do not believe they put by one penny out
of their good wages, but they like to have a
little money always in hand to spend, and
much prefer this system of payments to a
share in the crop or to being paid in a lump
at the end of the year. I have tried all three
plans, and do not hesitate to say this is the
best. And so, with good management, good
wages paid regularly, and no outside interference, there need be no trouble whatever
with Southern labour. But of the three I consider outside interference by far the worst evil
Southern planters have to contend against.

The negroes are so like children, so un-
reasoning and easily influenced, that they are
led away by any promise that sounds fair, or
inducement which is offered. And although
I confidently assert that nowhere in the world
are agricultural labourers in a better condition, or better paid, than our negroes, and
that though for twelve years they have been

well paid, and never have known us to break
our promises to them, yet I am perfectly sure
that if anyone should visit Butler's Island to-
morrow, absolute stranger though he might
be, and promise the negroes houses, or land,
or riches in Kansas or in Timbuctoo, they
would leave us without a moment's hesitation,
or doubt in their new friend's trustworthiness,
just as my child might be tempted away from
me by any stranger who promised her a new
toy.   Children they are in their nature and
character, and children they will remain until
the end of the chapter.

> Oh, bruders, let us leave
> Dis buckra land for Hayti,
> Dah we be receive
> Grand as Lafayetty.
> Make a mighty show
> When we land from steamship,
> You'll be like Monro,
> Me like Lewis Philip.
>
> O dat equal sod,
> Who not want to go-y,
> Dah we feel no rod,
> Dah we hab no foe-y,

Dah we lib so fine,
Dah hab coach and horsey,
Ebbry day we dine,
We hab tree, four coursey.

No more our son cry sweep,
No more he play de lackey,
No more our daughters weep,
'Kase dey call dem blacky.
No more dey servants be,
No more dey scrub and cook-y,
But ebbry day we'll see
Dem read de novel book-y.

Dah we sure to make
Our daughter de fine lady,
Dat dey husbands take
'Bove de common grady ;
And perhaps our son
He rise in glory splendour,
Be like Washington,
His country's brave defender.' [1]

Put Kansas for Hayti, and 1879 for 1840,
and haven't we exactly the same story ?

[1] This delightful song was composed somewhere about
1840, at the time of one of the Haytian revolutions, when the
negroes, imagining that they would have no more work to do,
but all be ladies and gentlemen, took the most absurd airs,
and went about calling themselves by all the different distinguished names they had ever heard.

ADDENDA.

—⋄—

HAVING written the foregoing pages some years ago, and having just returned from another visit to the South, after an absence of six years, I cannot refrain from adding a few words with regard to the condition of the negroes now and formerly, and their own manner of speaking of their condition as slaves. The question whether slavery is or is not a moral wrong I do not wish or intend to discuss; but in urging the injustice of requiring labour from people to whom no wages were paid, which was formerly one of the charges brought against the masters, it seems strange that wages were always thought of as mere money payments, and the fact that the negroes were fed, clothed, and housed at their masters' expense was never taken into account as wages, although often taking more money out of the owner's pocket than if the ordinary labourers' wages had been paid in hard money. Besides these items, a doctor's services were furnished, one being paid a certain yearly salary for visiting the plantation, three times a week I think it was, and of course all medicines were given to them free of charge. They were, besides, allowed to raise poultry to sell, and chickens, eggs, and the pretty baskets they used to make often brought the industrious ones in a nice little income of their own. At Christmas all the head men received a present of money, some being as high as ten pounds, and every deserving negro was similarly rewarded.

These facts I learned accidentally in looking over the old plantation books which fell into my hands about a year ago. I also found from old letters how particular the owners always were to have the best goods furnished for the people's clothing. The winter material was a heavy woollen cloth called Welsh plains, which was imported from England, and many of the letters contained apologies and explanations from the Liverpool firm who furnished the goods about the quality, which had evidently been found fault with. The character of the goods was also confirmed by the testimony of the negroes themselves, my housemaid saying one day *à propos* of the heavy blankets on my bed, ' Ah, in de old time we hab blankets like dese gib to us, but now we can only buy such poor ones dey no good at all ; ' and another, not one of our people, meeting us in a shop in Darien, turned from the rather flimsy cloth he was bargaining for, and taking hold of the dark blue tweed of my husband's coat, said, ' Sar, ware you git dis stuff? We used to git dis kind before the war, but now we neber sees it.'

Two extracts from letters written by

former agents to my great-uncle about the
negroes bear such strong testimony to the
way in which the slaves were thought of,
spoken of, and treated ' in de old time,' that
I cannot resist copying them, especially
as it was with a feeling of real pleasure
that I read them myself. One was written in
1827 and the other in 1828.

In the first the overseer writes : ' I killed
twenty-eight head of beef for the people's
Christmas dinner. I can do more with them in
this way than if all the hides of the cattle were
made into lashes !' In the other he says, ' You
justly observe that if punishment is in one
hand, reward should be in the other. There
is but one way of managing negroes, particularly with so large a gang as I have to do
with, and many of them in point of intellect
far superior to the mass of common whites
about us. A faithful distribution of rewards
and punishments, and different modes of
punishment ; not always resorting to the lash,
but confinement at home, cutting short some

privilege, and never inflicting punishment without regular trial. We save many tons of rice by giving one to each driver ; it makes them active and watchful.'

So much for their treatment as slaves, and surely food, clothing, medicine and medical attendance, to say nothing of the twenty-eight head of beef killed for their Christmas dinner, might justly be regarded as wages or an equivalent for their labour. It is quite true they were not free to leave the place or choose their masters, but, until a very few years ago, were the majority of English labourers able to change their places or better their condition ? Far less well off in point of food, clothing, and houses, the low wages and large families of the English labourer tied him to the soil as effectually as ever slavery did the negroes ; and I doubt our slaves being willing to change places with the free English labourer of those days, had the change been offered him.

Now with regard to their own views

regarding their condition. They were always represented, and supposed to be by the Abolitionists, as pining for freedom, thirsting for education, and breaking their hearts over ill-treatment, separation from their children, and so on. Now in answer to this, which still stands as a reproach against those who ever owned slaves, I give one or two stories from the lips of the negroes themselves, and also a few facts of the present state of things *twenty* years after the emancipation of the slaves.

One of our former drivers was robbed by one of the other negroes of two hundred dollars he had laid by, and in speaking of it he said with a sigh, ' Ah, missus, in de ole time de people work all day and sleep all night, and hab no time for 'teal ; ' evidently thinking that state better than the present condition of freedom to be idle, and its natural consequence, dishonesty. Another poor old man, who had had his house burnt down and lost all his little savings, chickens, and pigs, happened to mention that his wife had died shortly before. I had not heard it, and told him so, expressing my sorrow at the same time. ' You didn't know it, missus ! ' said the old man, in a tone of indignant surprise. ' Ah, tings different now from de ole times; den if any of de people die, de oberseer hab to write to Massa John or Massa Peirce, and tell 'em so-and-so's dead, but now de people die and dey buried, and nobody know noting about it.' Another amused me very much by regretting that he was no longer allowed to correct the young people indiscriminately, and said that formerly if you ' flogged de children de parents much obliged to you, but now de young people 'lowed to grow up wid no principle.'

One old man, who had been sold many years ago, had found his way back after all this time to the old home, and was full of affectionate gratitude at being allowed once more to see us. When I said, ' I hope you found some of your own people left, Bristol,' he said,

' I not come to see dem, missus, I come to see my ole massa's family, and it rejoiced my heart to see you and dear little missus.'

These it may be said are the old people, but I found the young ones had just the same feeling of belonging to the same place and family as their fathers, constantly saying, when I met them off the place and did not recognise them, ' We your people, missus ; ' and these, many of them, were not even born in slavery, and were not working for us now.

So much for their own feeling as regards their past condition of servitude. I don't for one moment pretend that they would willingly return to slavery, any more than we would have them slaves again, but I merely give these instances to show that they did not suffer under the system or regard it with the horror they were supposed to do by all the advocates of abolition.

Now for their present moral, physical, and intellectual condition, their own people will tell you of each other, that they will not

only steal money when they get the chance,
but their neighbours' poultry, and in fact
nearly all they can lay their hands on. Yet
before the war absolute confidence was
placed in their trustworthiness, and that we
were justified in so doing will be seen by
some stories I have told in the foregoing
pages, of their faithful guardianship of our
property, and even money, during the trying
war times.

Formerly, the race was a most prolific
one, and ten or fifteen children a common
number to a family ; now two or three seem
to be the usual allowance, and many of the
young women at whose weddings I had
assisted ten years or so ago, in answer to
my question, ' Have you any children ? ' would
answer, ' I had ' one, two, or three, as the
case might be, ' but dey all dead.' Always
inclined to be immoral, they have now
thrown all semblance of chastity to the
winds, and when I said to my old nurse
how shocked and grieved I was to find how

ill-conducted the young girls were, so much worse than they used to be, she said, ' Missus, dere not one decent gal left in de place.' Their thirst for knowledge, which made young and old go to school as soon as the war was over, seems to have been quenched entirely, for, with one or two laudable exceptions, no one sends even their children to school now, and soon we shall have to introduce compulsory education. The only two negroes on the place who can write and add up accounts are the one we had educated at the North, and the one we had in England for three years. And yet it is twenty years since they were freed, and have been their own masters.

What has become of their longing for better things, and what is to become of them, poor people, ignorant and degraded as they are, and, so far as one can see, becoming more and more so ? As far as the masters are concerned, they are far better off—relieved from the terrible load of responsibility which slavery entailed, and I have always been thankful that before the property came into my hands, the slaves were freed. But for the negroes, I cannot help thinking things are worse than when they were disciplined and controlled by a superior race, notwithstanding the drawbacks to the system, and, in some cases, grave abuses attending it. If slavery made a Legree, it also made an Uncle Tom.

APPENDIX.

——◦•◦——

No. 1.

OUR ISLAND HOME.

Butler's Island, Georgia.

Dear E——, I feel anxious to tell you, as you no doubt also will be ready to learn, something concerning our island home in the South. Here we are then, safely settled down on a rice plantation in Georgia, about 4,000 miles away from our friends on your side of the water, and yet hearing every day the same language spoken, although it must be confessed in a very peculiar and hardly intelligible manner, by our sable brethren (I believe ' brethren ' is the proper term in these free and enlightened days).

I am monarch of all I survey, which is an
island of about 1,600 acres, surrounded by a
muddy-looking river, called by the romantic-
sounding Indian name of the Altamaha.
How far prettier these Indian names are
than our Anglo-Saxon. Take for instance,
Chicago, Indiana, Ogeechee, Cincinnati,
Omaha, &c. ; and what a pity they did not in
every case retain the old names, and call New
York Manhattan, which it really is.

Our castle is a neat but not gaudy little
frame house, with a piazza in front of it, from
which you descend by six steps into a garden,
or rather small grove of orange trees, pal-
mettoes, oleanders, and roses. The first-
named are laden with golden fruit, of a
quality unsurpassed anywhere in the world,
I am bold to say, for size and sweet-
ness. We are hard at work now packing
them up for market, and shall have over 100
barrels for sale. The interior of the mansion is in accordance with its modest exte-
rior ; a small dining-room, a small drawing-

room, a very small office or study, a small
hall, a pantry, and two comfortable bedrooms on the ground-floor, and two more
comfortable bedrooms over the dining and
drawing-rooms. At the rear of the house
about twelve yards, is what is called the
colony, where are situated the kitchen, servants' sitting-room and bedrooms, the laundry
and dairy, and in a corner of the yard is a
turkey-house, full of prime Christmas fowl.
Behind the colony is Settlement No. 1,
where the coloured people (I believe this
also is the correct term) reside. It consists
of an avenue of orange trees, on each side of
which are rows of wooden houses, and at the
end of which, facing the avenue, is what
was the old hospital, but which is now half
of it the church and the other half the residence of our English labourers, eight in
number. Immediately in front of our
garden is the Altamaha river, with the land-
ing-place for the boats, and from which all
the water-supply is drawn. On the left of us

is the overseer's house, a larger and more imposing edifice, although not so comfortable as ours. On the right are the barns and the new threshing mill and engine, which are very nearly finished, and present a magnificent appearance from the river. The old mill, with all the valuable machinery, was burnt down a year ago. The rest of the Island consists of rice-fields, of which about 1,000 acres are under cultivation or cultivable, some marsh land covered with thick bamboo and reeds, in which the wild duck do congregate, and some scrubby brushwood; also Settlements Nos. 2 and 3, an old, rickety, but very large barn, a ruined mill, a ruined sugar-house. Of the rice plantation and method of cultivating it, I shall hope to write at some future time when I know more about it. I shall also reserve my account of the liberated negro until I know more of him. I fear, however, that further acquaintance with that much-abused, and at the same time much over-rated specimen of humanity, will not tend to raise him much in my estimation. At present I have plenty to tell you about.

And first I must say something about our Church Services. Last Sunday we met, at 11 A.M., in the room which has for some years been used as the Chapel for the negroes, but which is small and not ornamented. I have in my eye a very good-sized room at the overseer's house, which I think I can make into quite a nice little Chapel. However, for the present we have to do with the little chamber at the old hospital, and here, on Sunday, I read through the service, and spoke to them on the subject of the Gospel for the day, viz., the miraculous feeding of the multitude with the loaves and fishes. I try and speak to them in as simple language as I can, as I fear they (the negroes) are very ignorant, although they have a minister of their own, and services twice a week. Concerning their religion and services I shall tell you more when I write to you on the subject of the negro.

I found them very attentive, and we sang the Old Hundredth and another hymn out of the American Hymnal, which had been taught them. Sunday afternoon, at three P.M., I had school for the children, but which was also attended by quite old people. We commenced by singing, then I said a few prayers, next I heard the children the Catechism and explained it to them, and after closing with hymns and prayers, we commenced practising chants and hymns. They are very quick at learning tunes, and I think in time we shall get a fair choir. Fancy a choir of small frizzle-headed little niggers in white surplices! We shall have to have a regular little church built first before we get to that. They have their own service in the evening.

I intend, as soon as we are quite settled down, to start a night school for them twice a week. Now I must tell you about a wedding which I performed last Saturday. The bridegroom was a grandfather, the bride a grandmother, both very respectable people.

The hour appointed was nine in the evening.
(It is quite the custom to be married in the
evening all through the United States.) The
little Chapel was crowded by a well-behaved
congregation of blackies. The bride, although
having reached years of discretion and
having gone through the ceremony before,
was as bashful and coy as blushing seventeen.
She was literally supported by her bridesmaid
(a lady of about the same age), who clutched
her hard by the arm as if she was afraid she
might escape. The bride's dress was simple
and neat—a white apron over a stuff gown,
and a white turban on, and white cotton gloves
on her hands, one of which held a white handkerchief, folded in the form of a fan or dinner
napkin in front of her face, to hide, I suppose,
her blushes, if indeed she could have shown
them on her jet-black face. The groom was
dressed in a sober suit of black with a blue
kerchief. When I put the all-important
question, ' Chatham, wilt thou have this
woman to thy wedded wife ? ' &c., the answer

was promptly given, 'I will, massa, I will:' and when I asked 'Who giveth this woman to be married to this man?' the father of the Island, old Angus, spoke out boldly, 'I do, massa, with all my heart.' The behaviour of all, however, was reverent throughout, more so than on another occasion, three or four years ago, when the old black preacher came over from another island to marry a couple, and was requested by their mistress to use the Prayer Book Service, which (although he was able to read) he did *not* understand. Consequently, he would read through all the Rubrics, and was going on through the Service for Visitation of the Sick, when he was judiciously stopped. J. W. L.

No. 2.

OUR HARVEST HOME.

Dear E——, —The 28th of November, 1873, will be likely to be long remembered by the inhabitants of Butler's Island, Georgia. Thursday, the 27th, was the day appointed by the President as the annual Thanksgiving Day, to be observed throughout the States ; and here let me observe by the way, that it would be well if our civil and ecclesiastical authorities in England would follow the example of America in this, and have one special day set apart for thanksgiving to the Almighty for the ingathering of the fruits of the earth. In the American Prayer Book there is moreover a Form of Prayer and Thanksgiving, to be used yearly on this occasion. Well, as I have said, the 27th was the day appointed, and we had made every preparation for the due observance of

that day, but the elements were unpropitious.
The rain fell in torrents, and when it does rain
here, which is not often, it comes down in real
earnest, and so we were forced to put off our
festival to the 28th, and were well rewarded
by doing so, as the sun once more shone
brightly, and the wind, which had been so
boisterous, sobered down, and the air was
fresh and balmy. At twelve o'clock we
assembled in the small room which does
duty for our church, which was decorated
with illuminated texts and branches of
palmetto, red cedar, and other evergreens,
while from the centre of the room was
suspended a big orange branch, laden with
the ripe fruit. The room was as full as it
could hold of negroes, amongst whom here
and there were a few white faces, the Englishmen we had brought with us, and the old
doctor from the neighbouring town, being
among the latter. The hymns selected were
the Old Hundredth, and the Harvest Hymn,
No. 224, from Hymns Ancient and Modern,

which were heartily sung by our youthful
black choir, all the people joining in the last
two lines of the hymn—

> For his mercies still endure,
> Ever faithful, ever sure.

At the close of the service I delivered a
short address on the object of our gathering,
and the necessity of preparing ourselves for
the great harvest at the end of the world,
Deut. viii. 10, 11. Service ended, we marched
in procession to the new barn, a youthful
black leading the van with a banner (which I
had brought with me from England), on
which were inscribed the words, 'The Lord
of the Harvest.' Behind the banner-bearer
I walked, and then the three black captains
or foremen of the gangs. After which, the
men two and two; and then the women,
dressed in Sunday best, and with picturesque
turbans on their heads.

The barn which was to be the banquet-
ing hall for the occasion is a large building
which has only just been completed, and

which consists of two storeys, each 60 feet
long by 25 broad. The feast was to take
place in the upper storey, and here great
preparations had been made in the way of
decorations. The walls were draped round
with old curtains, on which were texts and
mottoes. On one side, in large letters formed
of orange leaves, was ' Praise ye the Lord of
the Harvest,' on the other side, ' Welcome
to our Home,' and ' The Lord bless our
Home.' Along the base of the wall was the
fringe formed of the graceful fan-like palmetto,
whilst stars formed of the same plant were
fixed on each side of the texts. The cedar,
the cypress, the orange, the hickory, and
other evergreens were also brought into
requisition, whilst suspended from the topmost
beams of the hall were the Union Jack of
Old England, and the Stars and Stripes of
America, below which hung large bunches of
oranges and ears of rice, representing the
produce of the Island. About one hundred
coloured people sat down to a substantial

repast, consisting of stewed oysters, sweet potatoes, rice, rounds of beef, ham, bacon, hominy, oranges, and coffee, and it is needless to say that they did ample justice to the good things that were set before them. There were no toasts after dinner, as the fashion of toast-giving has not yet reached this part of the world, and probably would not have been understood by the sable guests. Dinner ended, we had, by way of sports, some excellent boat and canoe races along the broad river Altamaha, which flows at the foot of the barn. The way these negroes manage their small vessels is remarkable. The canoes are cut out of a single log of cypress, and each nigger 'paddles his own canoe' with great dexterity, using his paddle first on one side then on the other. The spectators were greatly excited, and ' Quash wins ' was heard on all sides, as the young, good-looking, dark-skinned carpenter shot past, showing his pearly teeth under his black moustache. The regatta ended, it was nearly dark, but the young people requested that they might shout for the new barn. This was not done, as you might be led to suppose, by loud hurrahs—much more systematic than that. The girls and boys assembled in the upper storey where we had feasted, and, having formed in a circle, commenced dancing or rather shuffling round (as they do not lift the heel), each one following close behind the other, and all singing as they danced a sort of dirge or hymn. As they continued they got louder in their song and more shuffling in their gait. It was curious, but not elegant. I cannot help thinking it is a remnant of their old country, as I have seen in Egypt a very similar performance, only rather more heathenish. Having finished their shouting, they returned peacefully to their homes, and so ended the first Harvest Festival celebrated on Butler's Island.　　　J. W. L.

No. 3.

CHRISTMAS SHOPPING DOWN SOUTH.

Dear E——, —Christmas shopping down South is a very different matter from shopping at the fashionable Spa within two miles of your house, and finding there everything necessary for your Christmas wants. Savannah is our Leamington, and is about 100 miles distant. Now, if we had the express trains of the Great Western Railway or London and North Western Railway close by, we might, at slight risk in these days to our necks, do it comfortably in three hours' time. As it is, however, the time occupied in getting to our shopping town is about eighteen hours, either by land or water, provided, that is, that the steamboats do not get stranded on a sandbank, or the trains do not break down in a swamp. Having several purchases to make in the way of knicknacks

for our Christmas tree, green vegetables for
our Christmas dinner, mules for our ploughs ;
and, moreover, having to see after all our
goods, which had just arrived at Savannah
by the steamer 'Darien,' after being three
months on the road, it was determined that
I should set out for the city of Savannah, and
the account of my journey to and fro is what
I purpose now to give you.   I was fortunate
enough to get a passage in the steamer of our
rice factor, Major W——, who had come down
partly on a pleasure trip and partly to get a
load of rice, and who had on board with him
the Bishop of the Diocese, a colonel, a naval
captain, and a planter, all of whom, together
with your humble servant, slept in a row
on the floor of the saloon or cabin, which
measured about 18ft. by 12ft.   Well, it was
arranged I should meet the steamer at 7 P.M.
in the evening at Darien, and I accordingly
rowed over there, but after waiting for two
hours, neither seeing nor hearing anything of
her, and supposing that she had either altered

her course or was high and dry on a sand-bank, I returned home again. I had not, however, been at home more than half an hour before I heard the whistle of the steamer in the distance, and immediately ordered the boat out with two fresh rowers, and set off as fast as we could go for Darien. Here I found her taking in fuel, and received a hearty welcome from all on board. After two hours' delay at Darien, we started about the middle of the night up the winding course of the river, and through the treacherous Romiley Marsh, where you can, in places, touch both shores of the land with a long pole. We arrived at Savannah without any mishap after twenty-four hours' journey, not reckoning the time I had to wait at Darien.

At Savannah I was hospitably enter-tained by my friend Mr. L., whose house I well remembered, from having received great hospitality there four years ago ; the beauti-ful garden of camelias was full of bloom, just as it was when I last visited it. Having accomplished my commissions, bought mules and ploughs, and had a long interview with the very troublesome Custom-house officers, and having, moreover, recovered my dear old retriever ' Toby,' who had been a passenger on board the steamer ' Darien,' and had made great friends with all the officers and crew, I thought I would try going home by rail, so I started at four P.M. on Tuesday for the station, or depôt (as it is called in this country), of the Atlantic Gulf R. R. Here I took a ticket for Jessup, a junction on the road, where I had to change on to the Brunswick and Albany R. R., and took ticket for No. 1, which I reached at ten P.M. I was assured by a gentleman on board the cars (whom afterwards I found to be an interested party) that I should find excellent accommodation at No. 1 ; but No. 1 proved not to be quite A1. It was situated in the middle of the pine forest, which stretches away inland for thousands of miles. A few wooden shanties belonging to the negroes showed that it *was* inhabited. To one of these shanties we, *i.e.*, three fellow-passengers (who had been beguiled into stopping there by our accommodating friend) and self, were guided by a small darkey with a lantern. We found the wooden erection was a store, where rice, potatoes, corn, calico, and whisky were dealt out to the negroes who inhabited those parts. The store was full of these gentry making their purchases, and enjoying themselves with dancing and singing to the tune of a fiddle. A large log fire burnt at one end of the store, and round this we gathered, waiting to be shown to our apartments for the night. After about an hour had elapsed, a boy came with a light to show us the way; he first led us outside the house, and then up a ladder which seemed to lead to a hayloft, but which really led to two roughly boarded rooms, not any better than lofts, which were supplied with beds, and not a single other article of furniture, the washing apparatus (which consisted of one small tin

basin) being placed in the passage between
the two rooms. Being an old traveller and
well acquainted with the customs of the
country, I immediately took possession of
the smallest room, and took my dog ' Toby '
in with me, thus effectually guarding against
any other companion in my room. The
other chamber, which was a large one with
two beds, I left to my three fellow-travellers.
This may have appeared selfish ; but *chacun
pour soi* is my motto when travelling in
unknown regions and with unknown friends.
I found the bed comfortable, although the
room was roughly put together, the lights
from the store below shining through the
chinks of the floor, and the sounds of music
and revelry being very distinct. As I was
pretty well tired by my journey, however,
I soon went fast asleep, regardless of the
music below me or the letting off of fireworks
outside ; and at six o'clock next morning was
up and got the first wash in the tin basin, after
which I knocked at my fellow-travellers' door

and awakened them. After a substantial breakfast of wild venison and eggs and bacon, we set off in a two-horse vehicle through the pine forest, to a place called Hammersmith landing, about seven miles distant, where we found a very small steamer about the size of a fishing punt, waiting to convey passengers to Darien, eight miles off. As it had to pass the head of our Island, I persuaded the captain and crew (who were one and the same person), to land me at a convenient spot, and after a walk of two miles across the Island, I reached my house at 11 A.M., having accomplished the return journey in nineteen hours. I may add that the results of my shopping were satisfactory, and that the Christmas tree exhibited in the new barn gave great delight to old and young among the coloured inhabitants of Butler's Island.

No. 4.

RICE-CULTIVATION.

Dear E——, —You would perhaps like to
know something about the cultivation of that
most useful of grains which forms the chief
staple of food for a vast number of people in
India and China, and through lack of which,
alas! so many of our fellow-subjects in the
Indian Empire are suffering so terribly. I
will therefore endeavour in this letter to give
you some idea of the way we cultivate rice
on Butler's Island. A plantation is not our
idea of a plantation in England, *i.e.* a pleasant
grove of trees : and a rice plantation is certainly not a particularly attractive-looking
place to the casual visitor, as the best land
for the purpose is the flattest, in order that
a plentiful supply of water may be flowed
upon it at different seasons of the year. It
consists for the most part of land redeemed

from the pine marshes, and a great deal of
trouble it must have cost those bold pio-
neers of civilisation who originally undertook
the task. Forests had to be cut down,
marshes drained, and a high embankment
thrown up round the whole plantation, before
anything could be done. Like the inhabitants of Holland, we depend upon our dykes
for our livelihood, and the chief expense in
connection with such property is keeping up
the banks and clearing the canals and drains
every year; if this were neglected for two or
three years, the plantation would relapse into
its original uncivilised state, and become
once more a desolate marsh, fit only for wild
duck, snipe, frogs, water snakes, and mud
turtle to live in. Hence the reason that, since
the war, owing to want of capital and labour,
much of the country in the Southern States
has returned to its normal condition, and
that whereas formerly, in six of the Southern
States, 186,000,000 bushels of rice were sent
to market, in 1870 only 72,000,000 were

raised. The original planters having been completely ruined by the war, the planting in many cases has been carried on by negroes on their own account in small patches. As the Agricultural Commissioner, in his report, has lately stated—' The rice-planters were driven from the Carolina and Georgia shores during the war, labour was in a disorganised and chaotic state, production had almost ceased, and at its close, dams, flood-gates, canals, mills, and houses were either dilapidated or destroyed, and the power to compel the labourers to go into the rice-swamps utterly broken. The labourers had scattered, gone into other businesses, and those obtainable would only work for themselves on a share contract. Many of the proprietors were dead, and more absentees, and inexperienced men from the North or elsewhere assumed their places. The rice-fields had grown up in weeds or tangled shrubbery, the labour of separation was discouraging, and the work of cultivation greatly increased, giving unexpected gravity to the accidents and contingencies of the season.'

This picture is by no means overdrawn, and even now, in our own neighbourhood, there is scarcely a planter whose plantation is not mortgaged, and whose crop is not the property of his factor who has advanced him money to plant with. They plant on sufferance, and live from hand to mouth as best they can. And now, to return to the subject of planting, operations may be said to commence towards the end of the fall, after the first frost, *i.e.* about November. The fields are first burnt off, that is to say, the dry grass, rice stubble, and reeds are in this manner cleared off; the ploughs are then put in, and the ditches and drains are cleaned out and the banks made up. The work of ditch-cleaning and banking is now generally done by gangs of Irishmen, who come down from the North each winter, and do the work admirably.

I ought, perhaps, to explain more fully

the configuration of a rice plantation. Round
the whole of it, as I have said, a high bank is
thrown up, to protect it from high tides and
freshets or floods ; the land within this embankment is divided off into fields by check-
banks and face ditches, and each field, which
is about twenty acres in size, is subdivided
by smaller ditches, called quarter drains.
Through the length and breadth of the plantation generally run two or three canals,
which serve to drain the Island, and also to
convey the flats, or large flat-bottomed boats
for harvesting the rice. Well, the land having
been burnt off, ploughed, and ditched, the
harrows are put on in early spring, and the
seed is planted in time, if possible, for the
first high tides in March. As soon as the
seed is sown, the water is let on to the fields,
and kept on eight or ten days to sprout the
rice ; this is called the first flow. About three
weeks afterwards the second flow is put on,
and kept on from ten to thirty days, and upon
the length of this second flow there is a great

diversity of opinion amongst the planters, some being for keeping it on as long as thirty days, in order to kill the grass and weeds, and others not keeping it on half that time, for fear of weakening the rice. The third or harvest flow is put on about the end of June, and kept on until the middle of August, when the crop is ready for harvesting : and this is work which can only be done by negroes, as owing to the swampy state of the fields and the great heat of the sun, the malarious atmosphere makes it dangerous for any white man to stay a single night on the plantation. The crop being harvested, nothing remains but to thresh it and send it to market. The threshing is done by a steam thresher, in much the same way as grain is threshed in England. It is generally, however, sent to the factor in rough, *i.e.* with the husk on, and is pounded in large mills at Savannah or Charleston, and is then ready for sale. The great enemies of the rice-planter are volunteer and freshets ; the first of these is the scattered seed of the rice, which becomes a very disagreeable weed, and is very difficult to eradicate ; the second the floods, which come down from the hilly country in · spring and autumn, and put the plantations under water, and the planters to much inconvenience. We have just had one of these visitors—fortunately, not a very serious one ; still it has prevented our doing any work for about a fortnight, and made some of the fields look like a vast lake.

With regard to our own labour on the plantation, we had at the beginning of the year seven Irishmen for ditching and banking, at two dollars per day ; an English carpenter and blacksmith, at two and a half each ; six English labourers, at one and a half each ; two coloured carpenters, at one and a half ; and about eighty negroes, full hands, three-quarter hands, half hands, and quarter hands, rating at twenty-four, eighteen, twelve, nine, and six dollars per month ; added to which we have a trunk-minder (to look after the trunks or locks which shut out the water from the ditches), a cow and sheep-minder, an ostler, a flatman, and a boatman. This seems to be a large staff for the cultivation of 500 acres; but we do not find it enough, as most of the negro hands are women and children, and the men do as little work as they can. We have fifteen mules for ploughing, harrowing, and drilling, and our wagons are large flats or punts with which the harvest is got in, whilst boats of various sizes do duty for light carts and carriages.

We have just leased a neighbouring island to an energetic young planter, who has brought down thirty Chinamen to work it. It remains to be seen whether they will do the work better than the negroes—they could not do it much worse. Our two small islands now represent the four quarters of the globe, as we have inhabitants on them from Europe, Asia, Africa, and America; and as for different sects, there are the followers of Confucius and of John Wesley, besides Roman Catholics, English Episcopalians, American Episcopalians, Baptists, and I know not what besides. The Established Church on the Island is Anglo-American Episcopalian, and there are no church rates. Last Sunday I had an excellent congregation in our new little church, some of the neighbours from the other plantations coming over to attend service. We expect a visit from Bishop Beckwith, our Diocesan, shortly.

The reason why the middle or sprout flow used to be about ten days and is now often thirty days, is because labour was plentiful, and all the grass or weeds could be picked out by hand. Now, owing to want of hands, water is kept on a long time in order to kill the grass, and so save trouble of picking. It is thought, however, by many, that the rice is weakened by being kept so long under water. In old times four to five acres was planted to the hand; now, ten acres and more are planted, so that we have only half the number of hands to plant the same quantity. Machinery has been introduced since the war, to take the place of hand-labour, so we have drills, horse-hoes, and carts as substitutes for hand-sowing, picking, and toating, *i.e.* carrying in baskets on the head. Much more might be done by machinery, but capital is wanted in the South to invest in it. Two and a half bushels of rice are planted to the acre, yielding thirty to fifty bushels per acre.

P.S.—We have just heard that a great 'freshet' is coming down from the up country to visit us. A telegram has been received to that effect; and it takes ten to fifteen days for it to travel the 500 miles. Although we have plenty of notice, we can do nothing to keep out the unwelcome visitor, and next week the whole Island may be under water, and all agricultural operations brought to a standstill at the most important season of the year. British farmers may be thankful that they have not ' freshets ' to overwhelm them, and negro labourers to vex and harass them.

J. W. L.

No. 5.

St. Simon's Island.

Through torrid tracts with fainting steps they go,
Where mild Altama murmurs to their woe,
Those blazing suns that dart a downward ray,
And fiercely shed intolerable day,
Those matted woods where birds forget to sing,
But silent bats in drowsy clusters cling,
Those poisonous fields with rank luxuriance crown'd,
Where the dark scorpion gathers death around,
Where at each step the stranger fears to wake
The rattling terrors of the vengeful snake.
Deserted Village.

Dear E——, A pleasant picture this of our country down here : but then Goldsmith never visited it himself, and was rather fond of drawing upon his imagination. In all probability he got some account of the wild Altama(ha) from General Oglethorpe (the friend of Dr. Johnson), who resided for some time at Frederica, on St. Simon's Island, when he was Governor of Georgia. It is a base libel on the beautiful island, and would not have done much to have encouraged emigration of the agricultural labourer of these days, under the fostering care of the great general. St. Simon's has witnessed many changes since the day when Oglethorpe first settled at Frederica in 1739, and called that wild spot after Frederick, son of George II. Charles Wesley accompanied him, and acted as his chaplain and secretary, while his brother, the great John, took up his abode at Savannah as Rector of Christ Church, the only incumbency he ever held. Both brothers were unfortunate in this first missionary enterprise of theirs. The reception of John at Savannah was most hearty, and the enthusiasm with which he began his work was great ; but, alas ! the enthusiasm on both sides soon passed away, and John Wesley found himself in difficulties with his people ; some say on account of an unfortunate love affair ; others, on account of his rigid adherence to what were termed his High Church views, and because he refused to administer the Holy Communion to the chief magistrate's niece. Whatever was the cause, he left Savannah after twenty-two months' residence, and thus ended, rather ingloriously, his mission to Georgia. He was succeeded in his work by his friend, the great Whitefield, whose labours there were more successful. Charles Wesley was not much more fortunate at Frederica : he found enemies there who tried, and succeeded for a time, in setting Oglethorpe against his chaplain and secretary, and by whom he was treated with such harshness that he left Georgia about six months after, and resigned his offices. The old oak is still to be seen at Frederica under which Charles Wesley is said to have preached the gospel. In justice to Oglethorpe it must be stated that he soon after found out that he had been deceived, and sent Charles Wesley a ring in

token of his friendship. There is a good
deal that is interesting in connection with the
Wesleys' brief residence in Georgia which I
have not space to write about, and I have
only alluded to them in connection with St.
Simon's. Frederica was in these early days
a rival of Savannah, and was fortified, and
the residence of the Governor of Georgia.
Now it has two or three nigger shanties and
one white man's tumble-down house. The
remains of the fortifications are still to be
seen, and the situation is a pretty one, on the
banks of the Sound. A great battle was
fought by Oglethorpe at St. Simon's against
the Spaniards in 1742, when the latter were
defeated with considerable loss. The scene
of action is marked by a place called 'Bloody
Marsh.' In later times St. Simon's was the
resort of many wealthy families, who had fine
houses, beautiful grounds, and flourishing
cotton plantations, where the famous Sea Island
cotton was raised to perfection. Fine hard shell
roads were made from one end of the Island

to the other (a distance of about twelve miles), and the gentlemen used to meet at their club-house to play at quoits and billiards, &c., or to arrange for a deer hunt or fishing excursion.

Great hospitality was shown, and open house was kept for all comers, whilst picnics and regattas were constantly taking place. The late disastrous civil war changed all this. The fine houses have fallen to decay or been burnt down; the grounds neglected and grown over with weeds; the plantations left, with a few exceptions, to the negroes; olive groves choked up with undergrowth; stately date-palms ruthlessly burnt down by negroes to make room for a small patch of corn, when there were hundreds of acres, untilled, close at hand; a few solitary white men eking out an existence by growing fruit trees and cab-bages, by planting small patches of cotton or corn, by hunting deer, or by selling whisky to the negroes. ' Sic transit gloria ' (Si) mondi. I made an excursion to St. Simon's, in company with a gentleman whose father used to have a fine house and large plantation there before the war. We started in our plantation boat from Butler's Island at six A.M., and rowed down the Altamaha to St. Simon's, a distance of about fourteen miles. After crossing Altamaha Sound, we entered Hampton River, which is really an arm of the sea, separating Little St. Simon's Island from its larger namesake. On our way we shot ducks, and an alligator that was slumbering on the marsh. How the monster did plunge and whisk its scaly tail about; but a charge of buckshot on the top of the rifle-bullet quieted him, and my companion boldly pulled him into the boat by the tail, where he lay quietly enough, although, I must say, I did not feel quite comfortable with such a fellow passenger, as I thought he might possibly revive, and take a piece out of my calf; but he had taken too many lead pills for that. We saw many of his comrades about, who were very shy of letting us come too near them; we also heard the old bull-alligators roaring like fat bulls of Basan on every side.

The first place we disembarked at was Hampton Point, where our land lay, and where formerly were a flourishing cotton plantation, a good plantation-house, negro houses built of tabby (a compost of oyster shells and mortar), a hospital, and other buildings connected with a well-regulated plantation. The residence was burnt down two years ago, the other houses are rapidly falling into ruin, and the sole occupants now of this part of the Island are old Uncle John and old Mum Peggy, a venerable couple who were faithful servants in the old times, and who have now reached the allotted term of man's existence, and remain as pensioners on the place. Uncle John has a fine face and a very pleasent manner, and is altogether about the best specimen I know of a faithful old negro, who has served his master well on earth, and is prepared to meet the great Master of all men hereafter. As for the place, I was delighted

with it : fine old evergreen oaks, with the
long grey moss hanging from the branches
like the hoary beard of some venerable patri-
arch ; peach, wild plum, and orange trees in
abundance, and in full blossom ; semi-tropical
vegetation and beautiful wild flowers, especially the yellow jessamine, which twines itself
in matted clusters amongst the tangled and
luxuriant vegetation ; whilst flitting about
were many-coloured butterflies, and the beautiful red cardinal bird. The Point juts out
between the Hampton River and a creek
which runs up about two miles into the
interior, and which looks like another river,
and along both rivers is a narrow strip of
sandy beach. What would not, I thought,
some of the wealthy capitalists give to trans-
port this spot to the old country, to form a
magnificent park for some modern palatial
mansion ; and here Uncle John and old
Mum Peggy have it all to themselves. About
a mile inland from the shore stands another
of the old family houses, now nearly in ruins,

which is approached on every side by dark avenues of fine ilex, or evergreen oaks.

After wandering about the place for some time, we started in our boat for Canon's Point, which is a mile distant, and separated from Hampton by the above-mentioned creek, the two points forming, as it were, a swallow-tail to the island. At Canon's Point stands what must once have been a very fine three-storeyed frame mansion, with a verandah running all round, and having a large portico on each side of it, whilst round it were vestiges of pretty grounds and gardens, which had once been tastefully laid out ; stately date-palms reared their lofty heads above the portico, and oleanders and other flowering shrubs were dotted about. My companion, I then discovered for the first time, had not been to his old home for sixteen years. What a change it must have seemed to him from the days when that home was the scene of unbounded hospitality, and full of merry children. There, amongst the tall grass and weeds, he could still make out the little garden which was the children's own, and from which he was able to dig up some roses and bulbs to carry away as a memento. There, on the old oak near the house, used to hang the swing on which the young ones were wont to amuse themselves; and there actually was the old negro woman, who used to be a faithful servant in the family, 'old Rina,' and was not she delighted to see 'Massa James' once more; and would not she do everything to make us comfortable in the old deserted house, although it had not a scrap of furniture in it; and did she not send 'heaps of howd-y' to all the members of his family?

Leaving my friend to recall bygone days amidst the scenes of his childhood, I attached myself to old Rina, and went off with her to the kitchen to see about dinner. She did not much like my interfering with the culinary department; but one dish I was determined to superintend myself, and it was

to be a 'surprise agréable' for my companion.
Our bill of fare (I cannot give it all in
French) was 'Scotch broth,' cold beef, duck,
potatoes, hominy, rice, and last, but not
least, *my* dish, which I shall call 'filet de
queue de l'alligator à la Altamaha,' and
very good I assure you it was. I had heard
that the tail of the alligator was considered a
delicacy, but had never met with anyone
who had actually tasted it, so I determined
to judge for myself. I cut a small piece off
and cooked it in butter, with plenty of pepper
and salt. I will venture to say that if it had
been served up in a Paris restaurant, with
spinach sauce, epicures would have taken it
for 'filet de veau aux épinards.' The meat
was whiter than veal, and quite tender. Altogether we made an excellent repast, and
afterwards slept soundly on the hard boards
of the chief apartment. Next morning we
were up early, and after a good meal of
hominy and poached eggs, started off, in a
mule cart belonging to one of the negroes, to

the other end of the Island, about twelve miles distant. The road, which was an old shell one, was tolerably good (quite as good as most of the roads which are to be found anywhere down South), and lay for the most part through primeval woods, which formed an arched avenue, and protected us from the heat of the sun. Here and there on the road were cleared spaces, where the negroes were lazily tilling the soil in a rough sort of manner for their own benefit. Many of them left their ploughs and came to us to have a shake of the hands with 'Massa James.' At St. Clair we stopped to have a look at the ruins of the house once occupied by General Oglethorpe, and which was difficult to find owing to the vegetation that had grown up all round it. We also stopped at a place called the Village, where stood a house belonging to my friend, and which was then occupied by two white men and their families, who seemed to get their chief living out of deer hunting. Here there were more friends of Massa James, and more hand-shaking. At length we reached our destination, a pretty place called Hamilton, situated on the sea-shore, with another house belonging to the family of my friend, and in which his elder brother lived a regular hermit's life. The doors and walls were covered with texts, and the young hermit was living chiefly on oysters and unleavened bread, and rendering the negroes aid to satisfy their temporal and spiritual wants. He was evi- dently quite a character, and I should like to have seen more of him, but we had to find our way over to Brunswick (having sent our own boat back), so we got three stalwart negroes to row us across the Sound in their boat, and reached Brunswick (thirteen miles' distance), in the evening, after having enjoyed our expedition to St. Simon's very much.   J. W. L.

No. 6.

The Emancipated African.

Dear E——, —The subject I have undertaken to write to you about is by no means as easy a one as might at first appear. It is indeed easy enough for a traveller passing rapidly through the Southern States, or getting his opinion of the negroes as Hepworth Dixon did from what he saw of the waiters at a Richmond hotel,—it is easy enough for such travellers to write a lot of nonsense about the intelligence of the coloured man, the mixture of races, miscegination, &c. But most travellers see nothing of the inner life and character of these people, and an American might just as well get his opinion of a Dorsetshire labourer from what he saw of a waiter at the Langham Hotel, as a traveller in the United

States form his opinion of plantation negroes
from what he saw of Eli Brown or other intelligent and civil waiters at the large hotels.
To know and understand the negro in his
present position, you must see and hear him
on the floor of the State Legislature, and
transact business with him on a plantation,
as well as chat familiarly with him on a pleasure excursion, or be waited on by him in an
hotel. I have done all this, and therefore
have some authority in speaking, and yet I
can scarcely say that I know the emancipated
African thoroughly yet.

The fact is the poor negro has since the
war been placed in an entirely false position,
and is therefore not to be blamed for many
of the absurdities he has committed, seeing
that he has been urged on by Northern
'carpet-baggers'[1] and Southern 'scalaways,'

[1] Carpet-baggers are unscrupulous men who rushed
down from the North after the war, to see what they could
pick up for themselves from the ruins of the South. 'Scalaways'—Southerners, who to serve their own ends professed
allegiance to the North, and betrayed their own friends.

who have used him as a tool to further their own nefarious ends.

The great mistake committed by the North was giving the negroes the franchise so soon after their emancipation, when they were not the least prepared for it. In 1865 Slavery was abolished, and no one even among the Southerners, I venture to say, would wish it back. In 1868 they were declared citizens of the United States, and in 1870 they had the right of voting given them, and at the same time persons concerned in the rebellion were excluded from public trusts by what was called the ' iron-clad ' oath ; and as if this was not enough, last year the Civil Rights Bill was passed, by which negroes were to be placed on a perfect equality with whites, who were to be compelled to travel in the same cars with them, and to send their children to the same schools. The consequence of all this is that where there is a majority of negroes, as is the case in the States of Louisiana, Mississippi, and South

Carolina, these States are placed completely
under negro rule, and scenes occur in the
State Legislatures which baffle description.
I recollect at the beginning of 1870 being at
Montgomery, the capital of Alabama, and
paying a visit to the State House there when
a discussion was going on with respect to a
large grant which was to be made for the
building of the Alabama and Chattanooga
Railway, the real object of which was to
put money into the pockets of certain carpet-
baggers, who, in order to gain their object
had bribed all the negroes to vote for the
passing of the Bill.   The scene was an exciting one. Several negro members were present,
with their legs stuck up on the desks in front
of them, and spitting all about them in free
and independent fashion.   One gentleman
having spoken for some time against the Bill,
and having reiterated his condemnation of it
as a fraudulent speculation, a stout negro
member for Mobile sprung up and said,
' Mister Speaker, when yesterday I spoke, I

was not allowed to go on because you said I spoke twice on same subject. Now what is sauce for the goose is sauce for the gander. Dis member is saying over and over again de same thing ; why don't you tell him to sit down ? for what is sauce for ' &c. To which the Speaker said, ' Sit down yourself, sir.' Another member (a carpet-bagger) jumped up and shook his fist in the speaking member's face, and told him he was a liar, and if he would come outside he would give him satisfaction.

This is nothing, however, to what has been going on in South Carolina this last session. Poor South Carolina, formerly the proudest State in America, boasting of her ancient families, remarkable for her wealth, culture, and refinement, now prostrate in the dust, ruled over by her former slaves, an old aristocratic society replaced by the most ignorant democracy that mankind ever saw invested with the functions of government. Of the one hundred and four representatives, there are but twenty-three representatives of her old civilisation, and these few can only look on at the squabbling crowd amongst whom they sit as silent enforced auditors. Of the 101 remaining, 94 are coloured, and 7 their white allies. The few honest amongst them see plundering and corruption going on on all sides, and can do nothing. Here is a specimen of the oratory of the House of Representatives at Columbia, the capital of South Carolina, where formerly such accomplished orators as Calhoun, Preston, Hayne, &c., were wont to be heard with admiration.

The debate was on Penitentiary Appropriations.

Minort (negro) : The appropriation is not a bit too large.

Humbert (negro) : The institution ought to be self-sustaining. The member only wants a grab at the money.

Hurley (negro) : Mr. Speaker : True—

Humbert (to Hurley) : You shet you myuf, sah ! (Roars of laughter.)

Greene (negro) : That thief from Darlington (Humbert)—

Humbert : If I have robbed anything, I expect to be ku-kluxed by just such highway robbers as the member (Greene) from Beaufort.

Greene : If the Governor were not such a coward, he would have cowhided you before this, or got somebody else to do it.

Hurley : If the gentleman from Beaufort (Greene) would allow the weapon named to be sliced from his cuticle, I might submit to the castigation.

Such is one of the numerous scenes enacted in some of the State Legislatures in the South. The negroes have it all their own way, and rob and plunder as they please. The Governor of South Carolina lives in luxury, and treats his soldiers to champagne, while the miserable planters have to pay taxes amounting to half their income, and if they fail to pay; their property is confiscated.

Louisiana and Mississippi are not much better off. The former has an ignorant negro barber for its Lieutenant-Governor, and the latter has just selected a negro steamboat porter as its United States Senator, filling the place once occupied by Jefferson Davis.

I might tell you much more with regard to those States that are now in the hands of the negroes, but enough has been said to show the terrible condition in which these States are now after the civil war. In a future letter I shall speak more fully upon the past and present condition of the South. Georgia, I am happy to say, owing to the prudent policy of her people and the energies of a population in possession of a State rich in resources of every kind—industrial, commercial, and mineral—has been able to shake off the carpet-bag and negro yoke, and is in a fair way to recover her independence. Still even in Georgia, and especially in our immediate neighbourhood, a very bad influence has been exercised over the negroes, which has caused us no small difficulty in one's dealings with them.

We have just heard of the death of a certain doctor who originally came from Philadelphia, and who was the means of stirring up an immense deal of ill-feeling amongst the coloured inhabitants of Darien, over whom he had gained considerable power, which he used for his own ends. I trust his death may be the means of making the people more peaceful and reconciled. From what has been said, it will be seen that most of the difficulties that have arisen between the negroes and their former masters have been owing to the pernicious influences that have been brought to bear on them by unscrupulous and bad men. Naturally they are quiet and peaceful enough, and I do not believe that they would ever have caused any trouble if they had been left to themselves. It is only surprising that they have behaved as well as they have, and that there was no insurrection amongst them during the war. When the war began, the Butler's Island negroes were all taken by one of the overseers up into the interior, and immediately on the conclusion of the war they returned to the Island, although they were free to go where they would.

A gentleman in the South, who went all through the war, told me that a negro boy of his accompanied him all the time, and that on one occasion, when he was going into battle, he gave him his great-coat and a sword, to take home to his family in case he should be killed. After the battle the boy made inquiries, and it was reported that his master was dead. The boy set off straight home with his master's things, although he had many liberal offers from Northern officers.

Mr. C—— was not killed or wounded ; and after the battle got leave to go on furlough for a short time. On his way home he was walking through a Southern city, when he saw a strange-looking figure coming towards him, which on nearing he perceived was his negro boy, clad in his long military cloak, and the sword dangling by his side, grinning from ear to ear with delight at the sight of his master.

Many other tales have I heard of their faithfulness and attachment to their old masters which I have not time to relate. The fact is, they are very like children, not hard to manage if kindly treated, but very easily led astray by bad advisers. They were encouraged in the idea that freedom meant no work, twenty acres of land, a mule, a gun, a watch, and an umbrella; and it was some time before they learnt that it would be necessary for them to work to support themselves and to obtain the above-named luxuries. An old negro man named Bran, who used to live at St. Simon's before the war, came the other day to see my wife at Brunswick. The poor old man seemed much broken, and burst into tears on seeing her. He then told us his sad tale. After the war he had bought a patch of ground (about twelve acres) in the pine woods, on the mainland. He began well, and had a few heifers and some fowls, but of late misfortunes had come thick upon him ; his crops, which would never have been very good on such land, had entirely failed. All his stock of chickens and heifers had been stolen by the coloured gentry in the neighbourhood. His son had left him to set up for himself, and lately his old wife, for whom he had a great affection, had died, and he was left alone in his old age with no means of support. At the conclusion of his pitiable tale, he again broke down and sobbed like a child. J. W. L.

No. 7.

OUR POST TOWN.

Dear E——, It is some time now since I have written to you from this side of the Atlantic. Pray accept my apologies, and at the same time my good wishes for the New Year. As I have never told you anything as yet about our market and post town, I shall begin my letter with a short account of that interesting town, or rather ' city ' as they call it.

And first, do not confuse this Darien with the Isthmus of Darien, near Panama, in South America. The only thing approaching to an isthmus that we have is a strip of land which formerly joined two parts of General's Island, which island lies between us and the city of Darien. This piece of land had a canal cut through it long before the canal through the great Isthmus of Darien was ever talked

about, and was accomplished in this wise—so
local tradition tells us.   General Oglethorpe,
being with his soldiers at Darien, and finding
himself hemmed in by the Spaniards, who
had blockaded the river Altamaha above and
below the town, adopted a bold plan.   He
sallied forth at night, and with his soldiers
cut through General's Island a canal about
three-quarters of a mile in length.   As their
only tools were their swords, and the obstruc-
tions in the shape of cypress roots were very
great, it was a big undertaking; but they did
it, so we are told, and escaped to St. Simon's
Island, and the name of that canal to this
day bears testimony to the deed, as it is called
' the General's Cut,' and it is through that
cut that we have to row whenever we want
to go to market.   Whilst he was about it,
I wish he had cut it a little deeper, as, when
the tide is low, we get stuck in the cut and
have to wait for high water, which is not
pleasant, especially on a very hot day (and
Christmas week the thermometer stood at

78°), as the muddy banks and low tide are not picturesque or sweet. Having struggled through the cut, we emerge once more into the broad Altamaha, and soon find ourselves at Darien. It is not an imposing city, I am free to confess. It stands on a bluff, *i.e.* the one piece of high ground between it and Savannah ; marshes to the right of it, marshes to the left of it, marshes in front of it. Adjoining the city of Darien is or was the city of Mackintosh, which, however, never existed except on paper. I have seen the plans of that city, and it is marked out with wide streets, fine squares, cemetery, town hall, &c., but it never was seen except on paper, and has lately been incorporated with Darien. The site has a fine frontage of marsh and reeds, and very much resembles Charles Dickens's 'Eden,' to which poor Martin and Mark Tapley were allured by the glowing descriptions of the Yankee speculators. I wish it did exist as on paper, as we own the greater part of it. But Darien does exist, and has several wharves along its banks, where occasionally you may see the steamer from Savannah, or a sailing vessel from Liverpool loading timber. It was once a cotton port, but the cotton has gone from it to Savannah ; now it is a timber port, and last year did a lively business. This year timber is dull, as the market in Europe is overstocked. The Georgian pine is considered the finest in the world, and therefore there will no doubt be a fresh demand before long. The chief port of Darien is, however, not at Darien, but ten miles down the river, at a place called ' Doboy,' and last year there were at one time over sixty vessels waiting to be loaded. Our leading men are the timber merchants, amongst whom are a Northerner, an Irish Canadian, a German, and a Scotchman. They have all come here to make their fortunes, and when they have made them mean to pack up their chattels and go off, as they do not find Darien sufficiently tempting to make it their permanent place of residence. Whilst residing here

they do a good deal for the place, and not
the least of their meritorious acts is the building of a Protestant Episcopal Church, which
they are about to undertake. It is to be built
at the expense of three of them, a Presbyterian, Unitarian, and Methodist. This is,
to say the least of it, liberal in every sense of
the word, and the sort of liberality you are
not likely to meet with in the old country.
I referred them to our friend Mr. Robinson as an architect, and they have received
the plans and specifications from the firm of
which he was a member at Manchester. I
think, from what I have seen of the plans,
that it promises to be an ornament to the
town, and the town certainly wants ornamen-
tation. It might be quite a pretty place if it
only had fine buildings and well-paved streets,
as there are several fine old evergreen oaks
scattered about it, and the view of the river,
notwithstanding the marshes, has a certain
wild picturesqueness about it. At present
the main street is a sandy road, with no

attempt at paving and no idea of lighting. On each side the buildings are, for the most part, wooden shanties of various dimensions. The only two buildings having any pretensions at all are the hotel called the Magnolia House, and the Masonic Hall, and both these buildings are of wood. They have had two fires lately, which have demolished about a quarter of the city, which, however, will be soon put up again, as it does not take very long to put up these frame houses, and it takes a very short time to burn them down.

A good many Israelites have found their way to this remote district, and it is whispered that their tumble-down shanties and Cheap Jack goods were very heavily insured, and thus both fires began in their quarter; and, moreover, that they were not losers by the transaction. Be that as it may, it is certain that the insurance companies have declined insuring any more buildings in the city of Darien. The shops here are unlike any you would be likely to meet with in your town, or any other town in England. They are emporiums of multitudinous articles; and although the articles sold are about four times the price and one-fourth as good as the same kind of article in England, yet the variety, I suppose, in some measure makes up for the inferiority.

The purchaser may go into one shop and purchase furniture for his house; stove to warm it, flour, groceries, and potatoes to satisfy his wants; medicines to heal all sickness, a fine dress and bonnet for his better half, toys for his children, ploughs, harness, and other requirements for the farm, and a drop of bad whisky for himself. The chief customers are the negroes, who delight in spending their money as soon as they get it, and who are not particular as to the quality or quantity or price of the article they wish to purchase, and who always choose the brightest of colours and gaudiest of bonnets for their womankind. Amongst other buildings con-

sumed by the fire was the Post Office ; and
the postmaster, a genial, accommodating, and
very important personage, was for a time
rather perplexed as to a temporary post-box
for the inhabitants. He has, however, solved
the difficulty, and now perambulates the street
in a loose coat supplied with large pockets
on each side. The citizens soon recognise his
genial countenance in the distance, and come
out with their letters, which they drop into the
receptacles of the perambulating pillar-box.
Talking of pillar-box reminds me of pill-box,
and this brings me to 'our doctor.' But I
feel that I cannot do justice to this old citizen
in the short time that is left me, and I must
give him a letter to himself, as he is quite a
character, and full of anecdotes about ante-
bellum times ; those good old days when
'the code of honour' was the fashion, which
meant that a Southern gentleman was scarcely
considered one if he was not prepared, on the
slightest pretext, to go forth to slay his neighbour or be slain himself, in what is commonly

known as a duel. Our doctor has the queerest-looking little wooden edifice for his office, and the most grotesque-looking negro boy for an attendant, that ever practising physician boasted of. But, as I have already said, he is worthy of a description by himself, and he shall have it. J. W. L.

No. 8.

'OUR DOCTOR.'

Butler's Island, Darien, Ga.

As you approach the city of Darien in a boat, your attention is drawn to a peculiar-looking erection, standing out alone on the edge of the bluff, and you begin to surmise for what purpose it may be used. It is about the size of a gipsy's caravan, but instead of being set upon wheels, it rests on one side on the bank, the side facing the river being supported by two posts or stilts. There seems to be a door on this side, but as it is about

10 feet from the ground, and has no steps up
to it, you come to the conclusion that there
must be some other way of egress and ingress.
From the river side it presents the appearance of a large Punch and Judy show, and
you can almost imagine life-size marionettes
going through a performance in the opening
which you mistook for the door. On a nearer
inspection, you find a board hanging below
this opening, on which is inscribed in large
letters, 'THE DOCTOR.' This is our doctor's
office, and probably you will see our doctor
sitting in a rocking chair at the opening,
smoking a long pipe, and scanning the last
paper that the weekly steamer has brought
down. On going up the bank and round to
the other side of the wooden erection, you
find the door, which is on a level with the
bank, and you there discern that the opposite
door serves as a window, there being no
glazed windows about the establishment.
Probably, in the doorway, you will find the
doctor's sole attendant, a hideous-looking

negro boy, marked with small-pox, and without shoes or stockings ; his position of rest is generally with his back against one door-post and his legs stuck up against the opposite one. This youth has been reared by the doctor from early infancy, and seems to have a sort of dog-like attachment to him, only he irritates his master not a little by insisting upon calling the people of his own nation gentlemen and ladies. 'Sare,' says the boy, 'dere is a gentleman outside wishes to see you.' 'What sort of a gentleman is he ?' says the doctor. 'He's rather a dark-faced one,' says the boy, and retires with a malicious chuckle. The boy's duties are devoted chiefly to attending to a lean shaggy white pony which lives under the erection and between the stilts, and which has to draw the old doctor about in a rickety old buggy. On entering the office you receive a hearty welcome from the old gentleman, who bids you take the only other chair, and offers you the pipe of peace. The office is about 12 by 12, with

few articles of furniture, an old stove that
smokes as hard as its master, a deal table, a
few shelves with empty medicine bottles and
well-worn magazines lying thereon. The
doctor is about three score and ten, small of
stature, with grizzly hair and a genial countenance, not much careworn considering the
many troubles he has had to go through, for
our doctor has seen better days, and delights
to tell the patient listener about those better
days, when the houses of all the wealthy
planters in the neighbourhood were thrown
open to him, and when he received a fixed
yearly salary from them for attending to their
negroes. Those indeed were palmy days for
the doctor, and he could boast of fine trotting
horses, elegant equipages, and a retinue of
slaves. Now, owing to the Yankees, whom
he does not love, matters are considerably
changed; he has hard work to find clients,
his only horse the old grey pony, his only
attendant the negro lad. Notwithstanding
this let down in the world, our doctor is still

cheerful, and can entertain you by the hour with tales of Southern life in former days, enough, indeed, to fill a volume ; and curious times they must have been by his account— semi-barbaric, semi-luxurious, taking one back a hundred years or more to the olden times of English society, when hard drinking and sharp duelling were the fashion. Our doctor has had in his medical capacity to be present at many a duel, and many a sad tale he has to tell of the fatal results. He never had to act first part in one, although he was on one occasion very near it, as he thought at the time. It happened thus. There was in the neighbourhood, a very eccentric old general who was a great patron of the little doctor's. The doctor, who passed off as a good mimic, was in the habit of taking off the general's eccentricities behind his back. This coming to the ears of the fire-eating general, he sent a note by a friend to the doctor, in which he demanded instant satisfaction for certain liberties taken by him, the nature of which would be explained to him. The little doctor trembled in his shoes, for he well knew the fiery temper of the general ; and, moreover, that he could snuff out a candle with a pistol at twelve paces. He tried to obtain some explanation of the general's intentions from the friend, but he could extract nothing more from him than that the doctor should attend the next evening at the hotel where the general was staying, when he would himself give the explanation and demand satisfaction. There was nothing for it but to obey, and so next evening the doctor went in fear and trembling to see the general, whom he found with a few friends round him. ' Sir,' said the general, ' I understand that you have been in the habit of imitating certain peculiarities of mine behind my back, and I sent my friend the Mayor to demand satisfaction of you for the liberty you have taken. The satisfaction that I require of you,' and here the little doctor felt his legs tremble under him, 'is that you forthwith proceed to give your entertainment in my presence, omitting nothing.' The doctor felt immensely relieved, and proceeded at once to do as he was bid. On another occasion he was on a visit to the same general, when the latter proposed a ride. A couple of steeds were brought out of the stables, one of which was assigned to the doctor. The general shortly appeared, with a vizor on his head and a lance in one hand, whilst in the other hand he had a heavy sabre, which he presented to the doctor, and then, mounting his steed, he informed the doctor seriously that they would have a tournament, and that he would use the lance whilst the doctor should defend himself with the broadsword. The doctor was aghast ; he knew not how to use the sword, and yet saw that the general was in earnest. There sat the tall gaunt figure ready to charge, just like Don Quixote, and Sancho Panza shook in his stirrups, but his remonstrances were only met by, 'Not afraid, sir ; I hope not afraid.' A friend who was by advised the doctor to fly, and he took the advice, turned his steed and fled, whilst the knight fairly couched his steady spear, and fiercely ran at him with rigorous might. Away rode the doctor for very life, with the general close at his heels, and never slacked reins until he reached a neighbouring planter's, when he threw himself off and rushed into the house. The fleetness of his steed had saved him, and he could bear with equanimity the reproaches of this modern Quixote. Many other tales of our doctor could I tell you did time allow, but I have given two specimens illustrating something of the manners and customs of the Southern gentleman in the days of his prosperity.

J. W. L.

P.S.—I omitted to state, in my account of Darien, that it was originally a Scotch colony, and was settled in 1735 under the name of New Inverness. The Highlanders from Darien, under the command of Colonel

MacIntosh, rendered valuable assistance to General Oglethorpe in his campaign against the Spaniards. Colonel MacIntosh was also in command of the Georgia Militia during the war of Independence, and greatly distinguished himself in his encounters with the Britishers. The county we live in is called after him, and the old family house of the MacIntoshes still exists about six miles from Darien.

No. 9.

A Trip to Florida.

Dear E——, About the middle of last month a looked-for freshet began to make its appearance at the head of our Island, and very gradually to flow over the rice-fields, until it reached our settlement and came up to the steps of the piazza. Higher and higher the water rose, and bit by bit the land disappeared. The cellar was cleared out of its contents; the negroes in the old houses moved their goods and chattels to the new houses we built last year, and to the uninhabited overseer's house ; our mules and horses were put in the rice mill, our sheep and cows were sent off to St. Simon's Island, and the chickens and rabbits had to get up into the trees. The water had risen 3 ft. 6 in. in our garden round the house, and a boat had to be tied to our doorstep to enable us to get away at all. The general aspect was not a cheerful one, and so we made up our minds to go away for awhile, until the waters had subsided. An English friend being with us, we thought a trip to Florida, the Paradise of America (I believe Paris is the Paradise of Americans), would be the pleasantest. So on February 18 we took passage on board the ' Lizzie Baker ' at Darien, and the next day found ourselves steaming up the St. John's River in Florida, and a magnificent river it is, the most beautiful in the Southern States. In some places half a mile wide, in others a mile, and sometimes as much as six miles broad. The water is of a clear brown peaty colour, such as you see in parts of Scotland and Ireland. The banks along both sides of it are fringed with woods of pine, evergreen oak, magnolia, bay, wild orange, palm, and many other trees, whilst every few miles is situated some pretty colony, which has sprung up within the last few years to accommodate the many visitors who flock down every winter to this semi-tropical climate, to avoid the bitter cold of a Northern winter, and who, leaving at the beginning of the week New York or Phila-delphia, with the thermometer at 20° below zero, find themselves at the end of the week transported to a Southern clime with Fahrenheit at 70° above o. Every year the number of visitors increases, and the large hotels, and boarding-houses, and steamers can scarcely accommodate the crowds. The first place the steamers stop at after entering the St. John's River is Jacksonville, a flourishing city, the great starting point for all travellers in Florida. Fifteen miles above Jacksonville you come to Mandarin, where Mrs. Harriet Beecher Stowe resides, since the war, in the middle of a pretty orange grove. Ten miles further is Hibernia, after which you come to Magnolia, one of the prettiest spots on the St. John's River, where some Boston gentlemen have built very pleasant cottages in park-like grounds. Green Cove Springs lies just beyond, and here you find a warm sulphur spring which discharges 3,000 gallons of water per minute, at a temperature of 78°. Continuing up the river you come to Tocoi, at which place you can take the train for St. Augustine, which lies about fifteen miles to the east. Passing on in the steamer by several pretty orange plantations, you arrive at Palatka, a thriving town, and from this place you are transferred to smaller steamers, which take you to many places of great interest and beauty, through a chain of lakes which forms the Upper St.

John's River. The sportsman finds his way to Enterprise, and from thence to the Indian River, the happy hunting grounds of enthusiastic hunters, in the waters of which are found endless variety of fish, turtles, lobsters, oysters, whilst in the vicinity of its shores are deer, wild turkey, an occasional bear, and many other smaller game. As, however, we did not get further than Palatka, it is chiefly of the northern part of the peninsula that I will tell you, reserving an account of the southern and less explored portion for a future time, if I shall be fortunate enough to explore it hereafter. I wish more particularly to tell you something of the ancient city of St. Augustine, the most ancient, the most interesting, and one of the most attractive places in the whole of the United States. The history of St. Augustine goes back to the time of Ponce de Leon, who discovered Florida in 1512, and since that date to the close of the late civil war, St. Augustine has been the scene of many a hard-fought battle and the stage of many a romantic drama. Thrilling tales and tragic episodes are told in connection with Florida, and this ancient city in particular. How the veteran cavalier Ponce de Leon set out in search of the Fountain of Youth, and expected to find it in the newly discovered and beautiful land of flowers, and to obtain a fresh lease of youthful vigour and enjoyment, which would enable him to gain the affections of a beautiful young signora whose hand he had sought in vain in his own country. How after many years of fruitless search, wounded in body, sick at heart, and empty of purse, he died in Cuba. How he was succeeded by other bold Spanish cavaliers, who were constantly rebuffed by the brave Indians of the country. How Panfilo de Narvaez was hemmed in on every side by the Indians, and almost starved to death ; and how the commander was lost at sea in escaping, and how few of his gallant band ever reached their home again.

Time would fail me to tell of Cabeça de

Vaca, the first discoverer of the Mississippi,
and the gallant De Soto, who explored Florida
and tried to reach Mexico, but struggled on
with his disheartened followers as far as the
banks of the Mississippi, where body and
spirit gave way, and he passed from this world,
second to none of his age in deeds of knightly
prowess.   Or of the bloodthirsty and bigoted
papist Menendez, who so barbarously and
treacherously massacred the poor Huguenots
at Anastasia Island, opposite St. Augustine,
and also at Fort Caroline, on the banks of the
St. John's; or of the terrible vengeance that
fell upon the Spanish colonists at the hands
of the Frenchman, Dominic de Gorgues ; and
how, later on, Menendez was attacked in his
fort at St. Augustine by our Sir Francis
Drake.   Are not all these mighty deeds recorded by the ancient chroniclers of Spanish
history ?

One tale I will relate to the credit of an
Indian maiden. Juan Ortiz, a follower of
Narvaez, a youth of eighteen, having been

captured by the Indians, was taken before a savage chief who was bitterly hostile to the Spaniards, and who at once ordered Ortiz to be stretched out upon a sort of wooden gridiron, and to be broiled alive. The cruel chief, Hirihigua, had a beautiful daughter about the same age as Ortiz, who seeing the dreadful fate to which the young Spaniard was doomed, threw herself at her father's feet and implored him to spare the life of the captive youth, urging upon him that this smooth-cheeked boy could do him no injury, and that it was more noble for a brave and great warrior like himself to keep the youth a captive. Her intercession was successful, and the young Spaniard was loosed, and his wounds cared for by the gentle hands of her who had saved his life. But some months later, his life being again in peril, his fair deliverer again came to his rescue, and at the dead of night conducted him out of the camp, and put him on the way to reach a friendly chief, Mucoso, who received him well, and protected him for many years from the rage of Hirihigua. What adds to the romance is that Hirihigua's daughter was affianced to Mucoso, and that owing to the latter's refusal to surrender Ortiz the alliance was broken off, and thus the fair Indian sacrificed her love to her humanity, and the brave chief his bride to his sense of honour.

No. 10.

CHURCH WORK AMONGST THE NEGROES.

Butler's Island, Darien, Ga.

Dear E——, It is with much pleasure that I indite this epistle to you to tell you about the happy results of our work amongst the negroes during the last two winters. Last Christmas I gave notice that, as the Bishop of the Diocese intended to hold a Confirmation at Darien in the early spring, I should be glad if any of our people who felt disposed to join our Communion would give me their names, in order that I might prepare them for

the Apostolic laying on of hands, and baptise
such as had not been already baptised.

I soon found that I had a very good class,
many of whom seemed in earnest about the
matter and attended regularly, and listened
attentively to what I had to say. Owing to
the good instruction that they had had for
some years, I found a fair number of them
knew the Catechism well, and seemed to
understand the explanation of it also ; answering, indeed, with more intelligence, I
must confess, than many agricultural young
people who have been prepared by me in
England. On Easter Day I gave notice that
I was prepared to take the names of those
who sincerely wished, of their own free will,
to be baptised and confirmed, and the consequence was that I had fourteen names for
baptism and twenty-two for confirmation.
As they had all been brought up in the
Baptist persuasion, I also gave notice that I
was prepared, if they preferred it, to immerse
them instead of pouring water over them, and

I gave them some days to think over the matter, having previously explained the reason why our Church, whilst it left the manner of baptising to the discretion of the minister, usually considered the latter method, *i.e.*, of pouring on the water, sufficient for the purpose. After consulting amongst themselves, they all agreed to be baptised by pouring on of water, and Low Sunday was the day appointed, and a red-letter day it may be marked in the calendar of our little church, for such an event as this had not happened before in our neighbourhood. On Low Sunday, then, fourteen black youths met me in a room at the overseer's house which served as a vestry, and from there marched two-and-two into the church, singing—' Onward, Christian soldiers, marching as to war.' The church was prettily decorated for the occasion ; the font, which was an extemporised one of wood and porcelain, was completely covered with our beautiful hanging moss, adorned with the wild blue iris and sweetly-scented tea-roses. On the communion table was a cross of moss and orange flowers, each side of which were vases of iris and Cape jessamine, whilst distributed about were more flowers, perfuming the air with their sweet fragrance.   The hymns sung were—'Soldiers of Christ, arise,' and the baptismal hymn, 'In token that thou shalt not fear.'   The behaviour of the youths was devout and solemn throughout.   After the second lesson I performed the baptismal service, and admitted fourteen young and promising negroes into the Church of Christ. At the close of the service I delivered a short address on the text, 'See, here is water ; what doth hinder me to be baptised ?' (Acts viii. 36), dwelling particularly on the fact that the Ethiopian baptised by Philip was the first individual convert to Christianity baptised after our Blessed Lord's ascension.   I also reminded them how, more than five years ago, when I had visited the Island as a perfect stranger to them, I had been asked to preach to them, and had selected the same subject, viz., Philip and the Ethiopian; and how, at the conclusion of the service, one of their old veterans, Commodore Bob by name, who soon after that was called to his account, had come up and shaken me by the hand and said that he had had a vision of Philip coming to him, and that there would be a great movement upon that Island. The old man's prophecy had, I believed, come true, although he was no longer amongst us to witness it. This was the movement, and it rested with them to show whether it was destined to be a successful one or not.

The following Friday, Bishop Beckwith, of Georgia, came to lay his hands upon them, accompanied by the Rev. Mr. Clute, rector of the parish; and a most impressive ceremony it was—perhaps one of the most impressive that I have yet witnessed. In addition to the fourteen youths that I had baptised the previous Sunday, there were six young women who had been baptised in the Baptist church, and one old veteran, Captain Angus

(our negro foreman), who was a Wesleyan.
We all met in our vestry room, and marched
into the church, preceded by a white banner
with a red cross on it, borne by a bright-
looking mulatto boy, singing as we entered
a favourite song of the negroes, the chorus of
which was—

> We will march through the valley with faith ;
> We will march through the valley with faith ;
> And Jesus Himself shall be our leader
> As we march through the valley with faith.

The church was crowded, not only with
negroes, but with many of the planters and
their families from the other plantations.
The singing was most creditably performed
by our coloured choir, who sang, besides the
chants, 'Soldiers, arise,' and 'Pilgrims of
the night,' and for a processional, 'Onward,
Christian soldiers.' The ceremony of laying
on of hands was performed by the Bishop
placing his hands on each candidate separately,
and pronouncing the blessing in the most
impressive manner. The address to the
candidates at the conclusion must have made

a deep impression on those just confirmed, as
perhaps there is no more eloquent preacher
or one with a finer delivery than Bishop
Beckwith amongst the many eloquent
Bishops in this country. His subject was
the laying on of hands by the Apostles after
Philip had baptised the Christian converts at
Samaria, and from this passage of Scripture
he showed how there were different orders
in the ministry, and whilst some could only
baptise, by others, like the Apostles and
their successors the Bishops, the laying on
of hands could alone be performed. On
Sunday all the candidates and many of the
old people partook of the Holy Communion,
the number of communicants amounting to
thirty-five. In the afternoon I went over
to Darien to witness the Confirmation of
some more coloured people, to the number of
ten, and had it not been for the heavy rain I
understand there would have been several
more. The service took place in an old
warehouse, but the negroes are now engaged

putting up an Episcopalian church for themselves, on a good site close to the town
which we have been able to let them have,
and I have no doubt but that when it is
finished it will be well filled every Sunday.

The work has begun well, and there is
every reason to look for good results.
Hitherto the Anglican Episcopal Church
has made but little progress amongst the
coloured people, and they have been left for
the most part to the mercies of illiterate and
often worthless Baptist preachers of their
own colour. The Roman Catholic Church
is beginning to make strenuous efforts for the
conversion of the negroes, and the Anglican
Church must not be behind in her efforts.
If she succeeds, and I believe she will,
notwithstanding the opposition that is raised
against her by interested black Baptists, she
will do more to civilise the negroes and to
make good Christians and worthy citizens
of them, than all the Fifteenth Amendments,
Civil Rights Bills, or Freedmen's Bureaux

that have been passed or established for his supposed benefit.

The negro, of course, is naturally tractable and docile, and is easily influenced for good or evil. Unprincipled men have tried to make use of him as a mere political tool, to increase the power of the executive party in the South : but I believe he is beginning to have his eyes opened to the real facts, and to find out that his best friends are the Southerners amongst whom he dwells, and who know and understand him, and who are ready to help him out of a difficulty.

P.S.—There are two churches for coloured members of the Protestant Episcopal Communion in Savannah. St. Augustine's is the High Church, and St. Stephen's is the Low Church ; for already, even amongst the coloured people, there are different shades of religion, just as there are different shades of colour. The High Church is served by Mr. Love, who is quite black, and his congregation are almost all of the darkest hue as to

complexion. His church is elaborately decorated at the east end, and bright banners
and May flowers and candlesticks are used
in the celebration of the service. Moreover,
he has a capital choir of small darkies in
cassocks and surplices, who performed Tallis's
full choral service very creditably. Mr. Love
himself is intelligent and well-educated, and is,
I believe, a British subject, having been born
and educated in the West Indies. He seems,
however, to preach rather over the heads of
his congregation, and not to be satisfied with
the simplest kind of address, most suitable to
the capacity of his hearers. Last year he had
fifty-five baptisms, twelve confirmations, and
forty communicants on his list. There are
good Sunday schools attached to this church.
The minister of the other church is Mr.
Atwell, and his services, as well as his church,
are of a simpler kind. He is a mulatto, and
his congregation are chiefly mulattoes ; he
seems to be a simple-minded, honest sort of
man, and anxious for the religious advance-

ment of his people. The Sunday I was there his wife played the organ, but the singing was not up to the usual standard of negro excellence. His baptisms last year numbered thirty-two, and the confirmations twelve. His communicants amounted to a hundred and twenty-one, and his Sunday scholars to eighty-six. He has a sewing class and Sunday School Library Association attached to his church, and has a special children's service once a month. The ministrations of both these coloured clergymen seem to be progressive, and it is to be hoped that in many cities in Georgia and throughout the South similar churches may be established, and as there are but few of them now, they are very much needed.

Yours truly,

J. W. L.

No. 11.

CHURCH WORK AMONGST THE NEGROES.
'AN EPISCOPAL CONVEYANCE.'

Butler's Island, Darien, Georgia.

Dear E——, —The Second Sunday after Easter was a day of Church rejoicing and festivity in two places in the State of Georgia. In Savannah the Roman Catholics had a grand festival on the occasion of the opening of their new Cathedral, which is really quite a fine building, erected by the coppers of the Irish, and the contributions levied at bazaars and lotteries, for the most part on heretical Protestants. Our Bishop received a polite invitation to attend, although he has been of late fighting them in their own paper upon the subject of the Pope's infallibility; but he, good man, was far better employed on that day, consecrating my church for the negroes at Darien, and it is about this consecration that I would

wish to write to you, humble as the ceremony was in comparison with the gorgeous
show that was going on in another part of the
State.

The day was most beautiful, which was
fortunate, as our roof was not completed.
The church was prettily adorned by the
coloured fair, or rather dark ones, of my congregation. We assembled at a house a
short distance off—the Bishop, the Rector of
the parish, six of the vestrymen of the parish
church, and myself, escorted by my choir
from Butler's Island. We marched to the
church, the choir singing, as a processional,
' Onward, Christian soldiers.' At the church
doors the Bishop was met by three black
wardens whom I had appointed, and the
senior warden presented him with the papers
conveying the church in trust to him. The
church, which is a roomy one, was crowded,
one side of it being filled with the white
citizens, the other side with the coloured
citizens, whilst in the chancel was the choir,

consisting of about thirty coloured singers. The musical portion of the service was very well rendered.

At the close of the Consecration Service, an admirable address was delivered by the very eloquent Bishop, upon the subject of the grand old African Bishop, St. Cyprian, after whom the church was named, and he dwelt with special satisfaction on the fact of St. Cyprian having, in the third century, withstood Pope Stephen to the face. After the sermon the Bishop confirmed nine coloured females, seven of whom I had baptised on Easter Sunday. They were all dressed in white, and seemed much affected by the ceremony. The long services concluded with the celebration of the Holy Communion, at which there were thirty communicants, almost all my last year's candidates being present. Amongst the communicants I was very glad to see the six white vestrymen of the parish church.

The Bishop expressed himself delighted

with the church, which has been entirely built by the negroes themselves, all the furniture for the interior being executed by them from designs I had furnished them with. The church is now consecrated, the congregation is formed ; a good deal, however, yet remains to be done, both as regards the material fabric in the way of vestry, porch, belfry and bell, communion service, font, &c., for which we want funds ; and still more yet remains to be done as regards the spiritual building up of the church—a minister of their own, a school of their own, &c., for which I fear they will have to wait some time. If only churchmen in the North would co-operate with those in the South, and instead of quarrelling about civil rights would recognise the fact that there must always exist a line between the two races, and that a social intermixture can never take place and is not advisable, a great work might be done amongst these poor people. A vast mission field is ready in which to work, into which the

plough has scarcely yet been put ; labourers
could be found to do the work, if funds would
be forthcoming. Churchmen in the South
have but little money to spare, and what
they have they require to rebuild their old
churches, and to pay the salaries of their old
ministers, which are low enough as it is.
Churchmen in the North express a great
affection for the African whom they have
freed ; they would do well to show their
affection for him by taking some interest in
his spiritual welfare. Up to this time he has
been the tool of political agitators and the
catspaw of a party seeking power. He is
very susceptible to good or bad influences ;
the latter in most cases have been brought
to bear on him, it were about time that the
former should be tried. The results would, I
think, exceed the hopes of many who are
doubtful about him.

I have alluded above to the low salaries
of the clergy in the South ; let me say a word
about our excellent Bishop, and contrast

his lot with that of the favoured diocesans in our own land. He has a diocese in size about equal to the whole of England ; he has no palace or pleasant grounds ; his salary is nominally five thousand dollars (1,000*l.*) per annum, but the payment of this is uncertain and always in arrears, so much so that he is often hard pressed to meet the numerous calls upon his purse ; his travelling expenses over so large an area are of course heavy, but they are, fortunately, lightened through the liberality of the railway companies, who give him free passes over many of their lines. He has to find lodgings in all sorts of quarters, where there is no wealthy man's house to go to, and he has to travel over the roughest of roads, often in the roughest of conveyances. Here is an example which has something of the ludicrous in it. After evening service at Darien, and some tea at Butler's Island, we started off to catch a train which was to leave ' No. 1,' on the Macon and Brunswick line at two o'clock in the morning. We left Butler's

Island at 9 P.M., and after an hour and a half's hard rowing got to the landing in the pine woods at 10.30. Here I had ordered a vehicle to meet us to take us to the station about seven miles off. Arrived there, we found no vehicle awaiting us (it had been and gone away again, as we afterwards heard). There was nothing for it but to shoulder our baggage and walk to the nearest planter's house about a mile off. On reaching the house there was no sign of life, the planter having gone to his home in Brunswick for the Sunday, and taken his buggy and horse with him. I sent one of our boatmen to the nearest negro settlement, nearly a mile away, and, after considerable delay, he brought a darky back with him whom I knew. After a little consultation he managed to get a rice cart without any springs to it, and an old mule, and having put plenty of rice straw in the bottom of the cart, his lordship and I started in this episcopal conveyance on a drive of over seven miles through the pine woods and over a road strewed with branches and logs. Of course we could only travel at a slow walk, and accomplished the journey in about two hours, arriving at the station at 2 A.M., in time, however, to catch the train. I forgot to say that, besides ourselves and the driver, we had my dog ' Toby,' a small negro I was taking North with me, and our baggage. I could not help exclaiming to the Bishop, ' Oh that I could only have a good picture of this party, that I might send it home to one of our great dignitaries in the Church, and show them how a worthy Bishop in this country travels through his diocese !'

J. W. L.

No. 12.

A FAREWELL PARTING.

London : February 1877.

Dear E——, —I was down South this winter alone for nearly two months, winding up our affairs there, previous to leaving the country, for some time at least. Many pleasant reminiscences of our Southern home will remain imprinted on my mind, and my connection with the negroes will be amongst the pleasantest. The fact is, that with all their faults there is something that attracts one much to these Africans, and if only they could be left alone by the agitators from the North, there would be little doubt but that Southern whites and blacks would soon pull well together. You may perhaps have read some very excellent letters which have lately been appearing in the *Times*, from its Special Correspondent ; if so, you will have been able to form some fair idea of the real state of

affairs down there, which have been hitherto
so much misrepresented. I see that in his
last letter, which was dated from New Orleans,
January 25, and which was in the *Times*
of February 16, he is good enough to
refer to a conversation he had with me at
Charlestown on the subject of the two races
in Georgia, and mentions a certain incident
which I related to him to illustrate the good
feeling which existed there between whites
and blacks. The full particulars are these.
Lewis Jackson, a black man, who by the way
has acted as churchwarden of the coloured
church at Darien, was put up by the white
Democrats of the place to fill the position of
Ordinary of the city, and he was opposed by
a white man who was chiefly supported by
the black Republicans. This would scarcely
be believed by men in the North, who
declare that in Georgia no negro has a
chance of office, and that no negro votes the
Democratic ticket unless he is intimidated
into so doing. Another negro in Darien,

who held the office of constable, not only voted for the Democratic ticket, but happening to have twins born that day, named one 'Tilden Centennial Guyton,' and the other 'Hendricks Centennial Guyton,' which I do not suppose he could have been intimidated into doing. The fact is the intimidation is generally the other way, and negroes who do not hold important positions like Jackson and Guyton are afraid to vote for the Democrats because of their own people. The Northerners take it for granted that every negro *must* be Republican, because the Republicans released them from bondage ; they seem to forget that since the war the Republicans have really done nothing for the negroes, nor in any way fulfilled the many promises they made to them. The Freedmen's Bureau has only striven to set the freedmen against their old masters ; the Freedmen's Bank, after getting hold of all their savings, broke, and they lost all they had put in it. The Freedmen's Mission has, with all its professions, done scarcely anything for their spiritual welfare, and they are still left in the hands of ignorant, unscrupulous, and immoral political negro preachers, who are mere tools in the hands of a party. On the other hand they look to their old masters for employment, and for any little help they may require. Is it to be wondered at then, that having been cheated and defrauded in every way by those whom they looked upon as their saviours, they should begin to turn to their old masters, who they find after all are their best friends ? They are called down-trodden, but anyone who last month witnessed in Charlestown their wonderful annual procession to celebrate Emancipation, which is so graphically described by the Special Correspondent of the *Times,* and which he and I witnessed together, would certainly have come away with the impression that the whites and not the blacks of Charlestown were the down-trodden ones. But to return to our own negroes, we parted from each other with many mutual regrets. On the last day of the old year, Sunday, I held two full services with them, with celebration of the Holy Communion, besides having a service and celebration for the whites at their church five miles the other side of Darien. The evening service I held at my own little Chapel on the Island, which was crowded, as several of my congregation from Darien came over in boats to attend ; they sang many of their favourite hymns, and the service was not over until nearly ten o'clock. After service, the night being a beautiful moonlight one, I took it into my head, as I felt rather excited after my day's work, to start off for our favourite St. Simon's Island, 15 miles off. So, much to the astonishment of the old foreman, I ordered the long-boat out, and, with four good rowers, we started on our journey. A most pleasant journey it was, the rowers singing their quaint songs all the way, whilst I lay wrapped up in the stern, steering. We reached St. Simon's at 12.30,

and so saw the New Year in. Arrived at
the Cottage there, we soon had a blazing
fire of pine wood, and I drew the sofa up
in front of the burning logs, and, wrapped
up in my blanket, was soon fast asleep,
whilst my negroes lay round the kitchen
fire, perfectly happy. Next morning the
St. Simon's people came all up to the
house to bid me God speed, after which I
wandered alone through the solitary woods
of this beautiful Island. The following
Thursday I held a farewell service at the
new church at Darien, and charged my
hearers to do their utmost to carry on the
work that had been thus auspiciously begun.
After service, every member of the congregation came up to shake hands and bid me
farewell, and I was much touched by their
simple, affectionate, but respectful manner.
God grant that they may have some minister
amongst them to take a real and hearty
interest in their spiritual welfare. I am sure
much can be done with these poor simple,

ignorant people. Whilst in New York,
preparatory to leaving in the steamer, I
went to see the secretary of the Episcopal
Missionary Society for coloured people, and
I urged on him the immediate wants of the
congregation of St. Cyprian's church at
Darien, and I am happy to say that I so far
succeeded as to get a promise from him
that the Society would send down a coloured
minister, and pay his expenses for six
months; this, at all events, will enable the
Bishop to look out for further aid. Now
that I am in England, I intend to make
personal appeals for fresh supplies to send
out to Darien. I might give you some
account of our journey home, but I am
afraid I have already written too much. I
will only say that we made a wonderfully
quick trip in the White Star steamer
'Britannic.' We were to have left on the
20th, but, owing to a fog, we did not leave
New York until January 21. The first
three days the weather was fine and calm,

the rest of the journey it blew a perfect gale ;
fortunately, the wind was with us and carried
us along.   We arrived at Queenstown on
the 29th, having accomplished the voyage
from land to land in less than eight days.
I saw in the papers that a steamer which
was going from England to New York had
taken twenty-seven days ; rather a difference.
The 30th, the day we reached Liverpool,
was the day of the terrific gale which did
so much mischief all over England.   It was
the first time that I had seen a really big sea,
and although these mountains of waves were
awful to behold, they were nevertheless very
grand, especially at night by moonlight.
On the Sunday I performed Divine Service,
and it was hard work to keep my equilibrium,
so I am not sorry to be once more on 'terra
firma,' and that terra my own land, Old
England.   J. W. L.